Making Magic

Making Magic
Breeding and Birthing a Healthy Foal

Leslie McDonald and
Meredith Weller, DVM

Half Halt Press, Inc.
Boonsboro, Maryland

MAKING MAGIC Breeding and Birthing a Healthy Foal

Published in the United States of America by

Half Halt Press, Inc.
P.O. Box 67
Boonsboro, MD 21713
www.halfhaltpress.com

Cover design by Sara Podgur Hoffman
Illustrations by Danielle Bartos
Photos by Doug Froh

This book was written as a presentation of the authors' personal experiences in horse breeding. It is not intended to be a veterinary manual or a substitute for professional veterinary medical advice. Readers are encouraged to consult with a veterinarian regarding all matters concerning the breeding and foaling of their horses. The authors do not assume any responsibility for actions that result as a consequence of the reading of this book.

Library of Congress Cataloging-in-Publication Data

McDonald, Leslie, 1950-
  Making Magic : breeding and birthing a healthy foal / Leslie McDonald and
Meredith Weller.
     p. cm.
  ISBN 0-939481-78-2 (978)
  1. Horses--Breeding. I. Weller, Meredith, 1958- II. Title.
  SF291.M33 2007
  636.1'07--dc22

                                        2007033148

To my husband and best friend, Doug, whose beautiful photography and unwavering belief in my dream helped to make it a reality.

Leslie McDonald

To Dr. Dan Stradley and Dr. Elizabeth Martinsen, mentors, friends and equine veterinarians extraordinaire, for illuminating this path; to my parents for a lifetime of encouragement; and to my husband, Butch, for his infinite patience.

Meredith Weller

Table of Contents

Chapter 1

The Journey

The journey begins as a dream, a hope, an expectation. The epitome of beauty and inspiration as defined by authors and artists throughout history. It is the opportunity to expand a relationship with a treasured friend and partner. It is the chance to create a champion to conquer new worlds, to carry you beyond imaginable horizons. It is the promise of new life, fresh beginnings and endless possibilities.

My journey began in a windswept field in Sjobo, Sweden in November 1999. No longer feeling the chilling winds that whipped my upturned collar, I stood transfixed by the captivating sight before me: A powerful bay mare galloped the perimeter of the three-acre field, her 5-month-old black filly striding effortlessly at her hip. The foal capered and fishtailed, squealing in pure joy at the run. They lapped the field twice before curiosity drew them to the gate where I waited with their owner.

And suddenly, before me stood Anastasia, tiny nostrils flaring. Ink black without a white hair on her shiny coat, her sides heaved from the gallop. The elegant, chiseled head and big, bold eyes were mirror images of her famous sire, Edinburg. Too shy to approach, she peered inquisitively at me, hiding behind her mother.

This was the conclusion of an 8-month wait. From the time I learned that the world-class Swedish Warmblood stallion, Edinburg, had unexpectedly died, I had wanted to find a suitable offspring from his

My first meeting with 5-month old Anastasia in the freedom of her home pasture in Sjobo, Sweden.

final foal crop. It was a desirable bloodline for me because I currently owned a talented 5-year-old gelding from Edinburg's first foal crop with whom I was delighted. I'd hoped my search would lead to a filly that would ultimately serve as my future broodmare to perpetuate the bloodline.

After 30 years as a professional in the horse business, I wanted to experience the full spectrum of the sport by creating my next dressage horse from the very beginning. I had reached a point in my career where I had the time and facilities to take on this project that had intrigued me since childhood. However, that commitment meant truly starting from scratch and educating myself to an entirely new aspect of the horse industry.

Swedish Warmbloods had been my riding breed of choice for 10 years, so another Edinburg offspring was very attractive to me. With the help of friends and agents, I had researched current popular Swedish Warmblood bloodlines, looking for the best combination to suit my competitive requirements.

EXPORT CERTIFICATE OF REGISTRY

Name: ANASTASIA Sex: Filly Registry no. 04-99-2568 Birth date: 10 June 1999.

Black,

Bred by Eva Sandberg, Ilstorp no 18, S-275 93 Sjöbo

Dam: Malva 18030				Sire: Edinburg 864			
Marsipan 15372		Happy Day 656		Disciplina		Elever	
Marine 12935	Ciceron 456	Sirikit 6855	Honeymoor xx	Ptitsa	Dokhod xx	Etelka	Vympel II (Vimpel)

Fourth generation:

Marcia 10042	Nepal 390	Adelitza 6361	Toreador 418	Novaja 5323	Afghan 277	Lorelei xx	Honeyway xx	Tsentu-rija	Paradox ox	Dolina xx	Kharkov xx	Teorema	Eksprompt	Mimiko (Mimka)	Velt

Fifth generation:

Mitzi 6651	Jovial 369	Daisy 4968	Polarstern 319	Adelfina III 4805	Biarritz 294	Santhussa 5854	Diogenes 311	Rolla 4397	Novarro 179	Floretta 3620	Effendi	Rock Goddess xx	Prince Chevalier xx	Honey Buzzard xx	Fairway xx	Trjasika	Tsent I	Strofa ox	Priboj ox	Remek xx	Ut Majeur xx	Gundline xx	Christal xx	Mechanika	Termit (Trak.)	Afischa	Eifel (Trak.)	Manka	Marcel xx	Weltawa (Trak.)	Polarstern (Trak.)

It is hereby certified, that the sire Edinburg 864 and the dam Malva 18030 to the above mentioned horse, are entered in the Swedish Warmblood studbook "Riksstambok for Svenska Varmblodiga Hästen", volume LI, and with original breeding and birth certificates are kept by us. Flyinge 23.3.2000.

Place and date   Registrator

The bloodlines represented on Anastasia's papers promised an excellent dressage pedigree that I hoped she would pass on to her future offspring.

In March 1999, one of my contacts notified me of the big mare in Sjobo who was in foal to Edinburg. The mare's sire was the Grand Prix dressage competitor, Happy Day. That combination with the Edinburg breeding meant that her foal would carry promising Grand Prix blood on both the sire and dam sides. I crossed my fingers and waited.

Anastasia was born June 10, 1999. Five months later when the filly was old enough to evaluate, I boarded a plane for Sweden. Now, as her delicate muzzle tentatively snuffled my outstretched hand, I realized how far my homework and perseverance had gotten me. As I reveled in the excitement of the moment, I never lost sight that for me and Anastasia the journey was only just beginning. The completion was going to require a lot of hard work, education and luck.

Keeping sight of the goal for my journey, I was advised by experts far wiser than me that the road ahead would not be simple. I was warned that circumstances, frequently beyond my control, could quickly transform the road from smooth and joyful to one fraught with disappointment and dead ends. Like all journeys, the creation of a healthy, sound foal is filled with choices, each requiring educated decisions and extensive knowledge. For the first-time breeder, access to this important knowledge often can be confusing due to limited or no experience with the subject.

Three-and-a-half years later, in the spring of 2003, I made the serious decision to breed Anastasia, now 4 years old. However, I was confronted with the realization of how little concrete knowledge I possessed about the science of breeding. From the time I was a teenager, I dreamed of breeding a quality mare to produce a top class foal that I could train through the levels. However, it was one thing to fantasize about contented, sleek broodmares nurturing capering foals but quite a different matter to turn those dreams into reality.

If you'd ask me how to ride a correct half-halt or how to teach piaffe, I'd have responded with a ready, confident answer. But if you'd ask me about the necessary skills required to breed my mare and produce a healthy foal, I was at a loss. I was a maiden sport horse breeder tackling the challenge of breeding a young, maiden mare. It was immediately evident to me that we "girls" were going to need as much experienced help as we could get.

Meredith Weller, a longtime friend and dressage student, was the ideal candidate to serve as counselor and guide for my journey with Anastasia.

Already a successful sport horse breeder, Meredith was passionate about the subject, exuding confidence and reason whenever we discussed the topic. She supported my efforts throughout every step of my journey from the initial decision to breed my mare through long distance phone coaching the morning of my foal's delivery. I benefited greatly from her expertise as she offered advice on techniques that she had honed over the years.

Meredith's initial horse breeding experience came when she was 16-years-old. Swinging aboard her Saddlebred mare's bare back, she rode seven miles down the road from her home stable to have her pasture bred by a neighbor's stallion. Five days later, she rode the mare back home, pregnant. Live cover and blind luck on the first try resulted in a golden chestnut with four white socks.

Two years later, her horses were sold to pay for college tuition. Graduation from veterinary school was followed by the creation of a small animal veterinary practice that sidetracked her journey with horses until 1995. That's when the dream of an employee in her office lured Meredith back into horse world with an irresistible idea.

It didn't take a lot of arm twisting to convince Meredith to invest as a partner in a broodmare to produce sport horses. According to her employee's plan, they would alternate ownership years and corresponding expenses. Meredith was to have the second year, which would give her the opportunity to experience the breeding experiment from the sidelines as an interested observer.

Although armed with enthusiasm and voluminous dreams, in reality the partners brought limited practical experience to the actual selection of the broodmare candidate. They canvassed magazine ads and placed endless phone calls until they located Suzie Cutie at a 300-horse breeding farm, specializing in the production of American Warmbloods.

The 10-year-old Thoroughbred mare had started an amazing 126 races in the course of an eight year career on the racetrack. Even though she was in poor physical condition, her solid conformation, proven stamina and big, searching eyes won the partners' hearts. Purchased in February 1996, Meredith nicknamed her Chance for "last chance."

The name was appropriate, for as luck and equine partnerships often go, the original partner who had brainstormed the plan unexpectedly diverted her focus to other responsibilities early in her horse ownership relationship with Meredith. What was to have been a watching and learning year for my friend suddenly became a year of sole responsibility. Thus the necessity for a rapid education into the science of breeding launched Meredith head first into the sport horse breeding business.

Seven years after her initial broodmare purchase, Meredith moved to a 35-acre breeding farm that she built from scratch, drawing on all the experience she had gained to that point. Specializing in the production of Holsteiner show jumpers, Meridian Farm opened its gates with its initial investment Suzie Cutie, her 5-year-old daughter, Neverland, and two other homebred yearling fillies. According to Meredith, she still eagerly anticipates the ups and downs that come with every breeding season.

When my mare became pregnant within the desired timetable utilizing Meredith's techniques, I was thrilled. "Your system is great. Have you ever considered writing a book for other breeding novices like me? You could help us first-timers eliminate a lot of the guesswork and mistakes."

"I thought about it," she admitted. "But I'm just not a creative writer. A few years ago a friend was going to collaborate with me and do the writing, but she moved away before we got past the planning stage."

Writing is my second passion after horses. I majored in English composition in college and even had a children's book as well as several volumes of poetry published. But it had been a long time since I'd come across a project that impassioned me as much as this. The opportunity to educate myself in the breeding processes while journaling the development of my pregnant mare and future sport horse was too good to pass up.

I didn't skip a beat. "Dig out your research material. You and I are going to write that book."

And thus, a long-distance partnership was formed. Meredith had been a regular student of mine at my stable in Columbus, Ohio, since 1998. When I moved to Cincinnati in 2001, her passion to continue her dressage education motivated her to commute bimonthly to my new farm to learn on one of my FEI schoolmasters. While she remained dedicated to her lessons throughout 2003 and 2004, our book project resulted in riding lessons that spilled over into long afternoon research and writing sessions that detailed the course of breeding, pregnancy and foaling. Month by month, as my mare's girth expanded, along with dietary and personality changes, we charted her journey through personal experience and expert advice.

Through **Making Magic**, we hope to simplify your journey by sharing the knowledge we have accumulated in the course of a truly awesome, fascinating year. Each chapter offers advice on one specific stage of the breeding year, culminating in the experiences of my personal journey with Anastasia. Through the presentation of an orderly progression of personal trials and errors, victories and light-bulb moments, we hope to help you make your own bit of magic in the creation of your sport horse dreams.

Chapter 2

To Breed or Not to Breed

Whether or not you should breed your mare is the single most important question you must consider before beginning your journey. The first reaction of the small, independent breeder is almost always emotional, either for sympathetic or romantic reasons. In order to be purely objective, you must distance yourself from your base emotions.

Be realistic: Of course you love your sweet old campaigner who has been with you since you were a teenager. And it might be true that she isn't too old to become pregnant even though her original job is becoming too physically difficult. Sure you visualize yourselves as inseparable soul mates, forever jumping countless fences, riding endless suppling dressage figures or bounding over coops through limitless fields. But, sadly, you realize that she is aging, and it's natural to want her to live on through her foal. So it's easy to convince yourself that given the right cross, you could free her shoulders, elevate her front end, correct her winging and set the competitive world on its ear with her offspring.

While the above scenarios may, at first glance, satisfy the illogical demands of a mare owner's emotions, to be successful in your breeding venture, you must set emotions aside and logically analyze *why* you want to breed. Horse breeding is a very speculative activity. Whenever doing anything speculative, it is good practice to weigh the benefits against the risks. In horse breeding, you have only one opportunity for success over the course of the reproductive year. Once your mare is bred, you are committed to the path you have selected; there's no turning back. Therefore, it's necessary to determine whether the possible benefits outweigh the risks before starting down the path.

In light of the expense, time and work required to produce a healthy foal, it does not make sense to breed without making logical, responsible decisions. There is a time to plan and a time to execute. Do your homework the year before you plan to breed to give yourself sufficient time to review bloodlines and evaluate potential stallions and their offspring.

The best rule of thumb is to breed the best to the best and hope for the best. There is no "super foal" guarantee no matter how ideal the bloodlines or how talented the mare and stallion. Chance still plays the biggest role in the final outcome.

The reasons to breed are endless. For every horse owner who decides to breed her mare, there is a special story. One of the simplest ways to tackle the question of "To Breed or Not to Breed" is to review the facts of your particular situation the same way a journalist develops a story: Seriously consider the who, what, why, when, and where of your plan. Only if these questions can be answered to your satisfaction and to that of an unbiased panel of friends or family members, are you ready to begin your journey.

Who: There are several angles from which to attack the subject of "who." Even before addressing the question of parentage, you must ask yourself, *who* is your market? Is the proposed foal to be a competition horse for yourself? Are you trying to perpetuate a successful bloodline that is in demand? Is your goal to set up a small breeding business and market your offspring to a specific sport horse niche?

Chances are the "who?" will fall into one of two categories: yourself or potential clients. If you have determined the foal will be for yourself, move on to the next question.

It is important to determine your market. Remember, you cannot be all things to all disciplines, so focus on a sport horse sector, whether it is dressage, jumpers or eventing. Study which bloodlines are competitively and commercially popular. This information is readily available from breed association registries, sport horse approvals and published competition results for stallions and their offspring. Would your mare's bloodlines and personal performance record interest potential buyers? Do you have contacts that will help with exposure when your foal is ready for the marketplace?

Be realistic about the value of your future foal and the amount of time you will need to keep and care for him especially if he has been produced for resale. Most potential buyers are shopping for a riding horse. Their dream is not to invest the time and money it takes to nurture a weanling until he has reached riding age. They are eager to be in the saddle in their quest to achieve their dream. Unless your breeding operation has an established reputation or your mare has previously produced an exceptional individual, your weanling will probably be a farm fixture for several years until he is ready to be broken. Be prepared for the time, expense and space this waiting game requires.

Once you have determined *who* is the ultimate recipient of your breeding efforts, you must next consider *who* are the most suitable stallion candidates to satisfy your requirements. Sport horse breeding represents a rare opportunity to access the best stallions throughout the world at a reasonable cost compared to the overall cost of the breeding endeavor.

Who is the stallion that is "Mr. Right?" Do you dare take a gamble on the "unknown factor" who is an unproven, hot young prospect just licensed by his registry with a limited production and/or show record, but with an attractive stud fee? Do you consider the older "star status" stallion who is at the end of his breeding career with diminished sperm motility, but a long record of producing successful progeny? Or do you follow the safer middle road, selecting an established stallion with popular bloodlines and a proven production record?

Another important *who* for serious consideration is *who* will you rely on to get your mare pregnant. How do you know who is the best veterinarian for your mare? Just because you have an established working relationship with your barn vet does not mean she is the best person to handle your reproduction work.

Veterinarians fall into three basic categories:

1. The *general practitioner* is a multi-species veterinarian who may handle both small and large animals including dogs, cats, horses and farm animals. Because of their broad range of clientele, general practitioners may have limited equine reproduction experience. If you decide to use a general practitioner, be sure she has the experience, interest and time to devote to your horse's requirements.

2. *Equine-only practitioners* limit their practice to the treatment of horses. Despite being equine specialists, ascertain that your candidate is interested and experienced in reproduction with the skills to deal with extraordinary circumstances that may arise in the course of the pregnancy. Your equine veterinarian may be a sought-after leg specialist, but this does not mean she is a reproduction authority. Veterinary specialties can be very vertical in nature.

3. *Theriogenologists* specialize in equine reproduction and are usually board certified by the American College of Theriogenology under the auspices of the American Veterinary Medical Association. A mare owner should seek out this type of specialist if she has an older mare, one with a history of reproductive problems or if she plans to use frozen semen or embryo transfer.

Don't be afraid to ask your veterinarian frank questions to ascertain their qualifications to handle the type of breeding you have in mind. A portion of the success or failure of your breeding venture is in his or her hands. No matter how well you have done your research or how glowing the bloodlines you have selected, a large part of the responsibility to implement your plan relies on the veterinarian's skill and experience.

Ask specifically if her experience is primarily with horses, as reproduction work with horses differs from other livestock. Does your vet have excellent palpation skills? Does she possess an ultrasound and have the skill to read it clearly? Does she have experience with artificial insemination or has she done primarily live cover as is used on Thoroughbred farms? If your vet is skilled at artificial insemination, be sure she also has experience in dealing with the more complicated requirements of frozen semen, if that is the method you plan to use.

Ask your vet how many mares she bred last year, and what percentage became pregnant on the first try. Also ask what percentage of the mares she bred stayed pregnant for the entire breeding season. Determine what percentage of all those mares were bred utilizing the same method you are planning to use. What percentage of those breedings resulted in successful pregnancies? For example, your vet had the majority of her success with live cover, but little or no success with AI. If your breeding plan calls for the use of AI, this is probably not the ideal choice for your situation.

It is a good policy to use a veterinarian who pursues continuing education in the field of reproduction. She should not be rigidly fixated on old methods that have a low percentage of success. Ideally your veterinarian should not be afraid to ask questions and reach out to more experienced reproduction specialists should a problem develop. She should be open to suggestions and pursuing alternative options if her first course of action is not successful.

Finally, it is critical for your vet to be accessible and possess good communication skills. The most technically proficient vet is of no value to you if she is unavailable when the Equitainer arrives and the mare is ready to be bred. A good working relationship will be dependent on her communications skills in returning phone calls and keeping you posted on the status of your mare. She also must be reliable enough to respond when your mare goes into labor. Ninety percent of all births occur without a problem, but you won't know if your mare falls into the 10-percent risk category until it happens. In that case, it may be too late for your veterinarian to rectify a problem if she's not accessible.

What: *What* is the ultimate goal of your journey? *What* type of horse do you want to produce? Creating a foal for the sake of creating a foal is not a sufficient reason to breed.

If you are planning to breed a horse for yourself, define your personal goals. Are you an amateur rider who desires a solid, quiet partner? Are you a serious competitor seeking a horse with the capability for upper level work? Do you want steady, comfortable gaits, or do you have the athletic ability and desire to ride "golly-gee-whiz" gaits that will blow your doors off? Are you a naturally tense rider who is better suited to a slower, off-the-leg horse, or do you want fire and razzle-dazzle from your mount? Plan your breeding to suit your physical requirements and competitive goals.

Step back and approach the question of *what* you want as though you were shopping for a weanling that is already on the ground. What criteria does that youngster need to fulfill to make you reach for your checkbook without hesitation? Be specific! When you can visualize the ideal candidate, turn the information back on yourself as the breeder given the responsibility to create just that individual. Only then is it time to consider your mare and stallion candidates.

Why: *Why* do you want to breed your mare? Is she truly such an exceptional representative of her breed and discipline that you could not do better by simply going shopping for an existing weanling with the bloodlines you desire?

Pride of production is a benefit many owners derive from breeding their mares. By experiencing the process, you will have the additional benefit of an intense bonding experience with your mare, which will hopefully continue with her foal. It is truly a creative process to match your mare with a suitable stallion to produce a foal that hopefully improves on the parents. Breeding also represents an opportunity to produce a foal that is mentally and physically sound to your expectations. You also may be rewarded for your efforts by selling the foal you have produced and seeing it go on to a successful career with an owner who loves and appreciates it.

When considering *why* to breed, you must be aware of the risks. Creative speculation among friends in your prebreeding days carries no risk, but when you actually take the step to implement that speculation and breed your mare, the fantasy becomes reality—fast! If you are the type of person who requires guarantees, take a big step backward and select a foal already on the ground that suits your criteria because there are no guarantees in breeding.

When making your decision, be sure to consider the high element of risk to the health and welfare of your mare. Sometimes even the best-laid plans and top veterinary care cannot save your mare and/or foal when things unexpectedly go wrong at a critical time in the delivery. It is difficult to be prepared for the emotional risk of losing the mare or the foal or producing a foal with physical disabilities.

And finally, there is the financial risk. While the stallion advertisements add fuel to your creative speculation of producing the "perfect" foal on a budget, the actual costs of your project can rapidly escalate when the mare doesn't conceive on the first, second or third tries. The collecting/shipping fees continue to mount. The vet's multiple trips to your farm make you think she should take up residence in your guest room. You feel like you should be named an expert on short cycling, but your mare is still not pregnant. The result is a very disappointing drain on your checkbook with possibly no foal to show for your efforts.

However, just as there are no guarantees for the fulfillment of dreams in the breeding of your mare, there are no limitations to the possibilities. Although the potential for risk exists with all breeding plans, dreams are what stimulate imagination to reach beyond the norm for something that is truly extraordinary.

Where: *Where* do you plan to foal out and raise your prospect? Can you see rolling pastures with safe, secure fencing and run-in sheds out your front window or is your mare kept at a public boarding stable? Do you possess the expertise to handle the foaling process? Would you recognize and know what to do should problems arise?

The consideration of where to keep your mare seriously comes into play when she is approximately 45 days from her foaling date. If you do not own a farm, your options are either a public boarding stable or a private farm specializing in breeding/foaling.

As your mare approaches her foaling date, she should be moved into a spacious box stall, a minimum of 12 feet by 24 feet. She should be under the watchful care of a competent individual who is experienced in recognizing the normal and abnormal signs of parturition. If you don't feel comfortable assuming this responsibility, discuss with your veterinarian the possibility of moving your mare to a professional foaling-out facility.

The foaling-out facility is set up for the sole purpose of providing a safe foaling experience. Your mare and foal will have immediate access to trained personnel experienced to cope with any problems or emergencies that may arise.

There are several drawbacks to a professional foaling facility: Foremost is the cost. You will pay a high dollar for what amounts to baby-sitting while your mare stands around waiting to foal. In order for your mare to develop disease immunity and antibodies to potentially infectious organisms, she should be stabled at the host facility no less than four to six weeks prior to her expected foaling date. These important antibodies eventually will be transferred to the mare's foal through her colostrum. In addition to developing antibodies, the mare also has the opportunity to acclimate to the facility and unfamiliar handling procedures.

If you are a hands-on person, you will have to surrender control of your mare's daily care and nutrition if she's boarded at a foaling facility. If your mare is to be turned out with a group of broodmares and foals, she will have to go through a socialization process. Finally, you must consider the risk of trailering a very pregnant mare to the facility and, later, trailering her and her new foal back to your home stable.

Whether utilizing a professional facility or your own farm, a suitable place to foal out should include generous amounts of pasture with foal-safe fencing. To understand what makes fencing safe, you must look at it from the perspective of a tiny newborn foal. One sunny morning the foal lies down beside her dam as she peacefully grazes the fenceline and, in the blink of an eye, she rolls beneath the bottom rail. The next moment you have total chaos as mare and foal panic while trying to reunite. Obviously, safe fencing is of utmost importance. The bottom board should not exceed 12 inches from the ground. True foal-safe fencing extends all the way to the ground. Another safety option is woven wire with spacing too small for a tiny hoof to slip through such as diamond mesh or no-climb fencing. An added safety feature would be a single strand of electric tape on the top board.

Pastures also should have run-in shelters for protection from the elements and insects. Run-in sheds should have adequate space with approximately 140 square feet per horse. The base of the run-in should be graded above the pasture for adequate drainage so the shelter stays dry inside. The shed should be built over a base made of drainage stone topped with crushed limestone.

When: There are many serious aspects to consider when asking this final question. *When* is the best time in both your life and your mare's life to consider breeding her? Do you want to ride and show your mare or are you willing to sacrifice time out of her training schedule and competitive career? Is your young, maiden mare old enough to maintain a pregnancy? Is your established campaigner too old to sustain a pregnancy?

When is the best time of the year to breed? *When* is your mare's fertility at its peak with the best chance of a positive result? Is your mare of a breed or discipline where an early-season birth will benefit the foal's future performance efforts such as in-hand futurities at breed shows? In that case, do you want to try to stimulate her early fertility with the use of artificial lights and hormones? Do you want a later-season foal but are afraid if you wait too long that your mare's fertility will decrease, lessening the chance of a pregnancy?

When is the best season for foaling in your geographic area? Will your new foal have access to turnout? Early foals have to contend with cold temperatures, wet weather and muddy fields with poor or no grass. Late summer foals have to suffer heat, hard ground and insects. In addition, late season births affect the foal's futurity status, putting it size- and maturity-wise behind the competition.

Personal Journey

In making my personal decision of "To Breed or Not to Breed," I gave serious consideration to each of the determining criteria, arriving at the following conclusions:

I couldn't wait to see what the future held for me and my two Edinburg siblings, Anastasia at 9 months and Horizon at 5 years.

Who: Determining the target market for my breeding project was the easiest part. The target was me! I was a serious professional dressage competitor, currently training my fourth Grand Prix horse.

My choice of broodmare prospect had been well researched. I purchased Anastasia in Sweden as a 5-month-old weanling, based on her conformation, bloodlines and my positive experience with an Edinburg son who I had purchased as a 3-year-old and was currently competing as a 5-year-old.

Anastasia and I had had three-and-a-half years to bond and grow together. As a 4-year-old, she stood a powerful 16.2 hands and was working quietly under saddle. In 2003, when she turned 3, I presented her at the Swedish Warmblood Association of North America's annual breeding stock approvals. At the inspection, the judges awarded her the top rating of Class 1, confirming, to my delight, that my broodmare selection had been an excellent choice.

The stallion I chose to compliment Anastasia was Vivaldi, a popular Swedish Warmblood standing at Three Crowns Farm in Woodinville, Washington. Vivaldi, who is now deceased, was a proven producer with many offspring competing successfully at the FEI levels in the United States and Europe. I knew several owners of Vivaldi offspring who confirmed their satis-

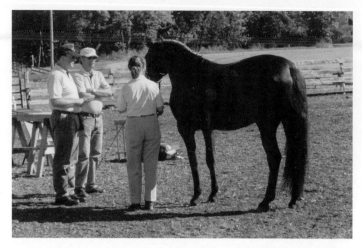

In 2002, I presented 3-year-old Anastasia to the judges at the 2002 Swedish Warmblood Association of North American bloodstock inspections in Burton, Ohio.

faction with the rideability, trainability and temperament of their horses. Although Vivaldi would be 19 at the time of the breeding to Anastasia, he still exhibited excellent semen motility with a high conception rate.

My regular farm veterinarian, Dr. Scott Strosnider of the Lebanon Equine Clinic in Lebanon, Ohio was qualified to handle the reproduction work required for artificial insemination by fresh-cooled semen. His experience combined with our excellent working relationship made him the natural choice.

What: My goal was to produce a competitive dressage prospect for myself with FEI potential. I hoped to retain Anastasia's temperament, trainability and elegant conformation that had received a "9" for type from the judges at her Swedish Warmblood inspection. In addition to Vivaldi's many wonderful qualities, I particularly chose him to enhance and improve the freedom of Anastasia's shoulder and the scope of her canter.

Why: After three decades as a practicing professional in the horse industry, I decided the time had come in my career to experience the full spectrum of creating my next sport horse. The creative challenge was to select bloodlines, physical type and performance capabilities in both a mare and a stallion whose combined breeding possessed the potential to create an FEI-level dressage prospect. Despite my training experience in the saddle and the competition ring, when it came to breeding I was a novice with the same dreams and hopes of all novice breeders. The successful completion of my breeding plan would require a lot of education and luck, but I was prepared to tackle the project with energy and excitement.

Located on 15 rolling acres in south western Ohio, I built Full Cry Farm to fulfill my dream of breeding and training quality Swedish Warm-bloods.

Where: Full Cry Farm, my home and 15-acre private training stable, was an ideal setting for the project. Anastasia had a large, walkout pasture from her stall complete with run-in shed. The pasture was constructed with foal-safe board fencing. Anastasia's 12-foot by 12-foot box stall easily could be converted to a 12-foot by 24-foot foaling stall by removing the partition that separated it from the adjoining stall. A video camera was installed above the stall to permit 24-hour surveillance from my bedroom television.

When: I had planned to follow the European practice of breaking my maiden mare as a 3-year-old, then taking time out of her training to breed her for one or two seasons before focusing on a competitive career. However, since Anastasia had been a late June foal, I determined she was too immature to breed in the spring of her third year. We broke her that summer, but delayed breeding until the following spring so the act of her growing a fetus would not detract from her own still-developing body.

After years of preparation and planning, I felt confident that Anastasia and I were ready to begin our exciting journey.

Since Anastasia's training schedule would not be affected by her pregnancy, I was free to select the ideal season when the climate would be most favorable for a newborn. Living in southern Ohio, I planned to breed for a late April or early May foal.

Chapter 3

The Best to the Best

"Breed the best to the best and hope for the best" is a time-honored horseman's adage. It is the best single piece of advice for the neophyte breeder. Do not breed out of sentimentality for a treasured partner or because you have a restricted budget or hear of a good-deal fire sale.

Although love may be the glue that has bound you and your current riding partner together through the years, it is not a sufficient reason to breed her. Look beyond the emotional attachment of her eyes, soul and shared experiences to consider the serious criteria of movement, conformation, temperament and rideability. If you were able to reproduce an exact replica of your mare, would you be truly happy? Do you honestly visualize that the offspring of this mare will carry you to bigger and better horizons? If the answer is "no" or a hesitant "maybe", then it is time to reconsider your choice.

Selecting the existing mare in your barn as a broodmare candidate is frequently not the best choice. Even if she has been a great companion, be realistic about her strengths and weaknesses. Do not scrimp on the mare side of the breeding equation assuming that a superior stallion will compensate for her shortcomings while retaining only her strengths.

Some hopeful breeders make parentage selections based on a fantasy notion that the planned offspring will receive the best of both parents, overriding negative characteristics. Breeders who adhere to this philosophy may also dabble in the production of "boutique breeds." These new registries spring up in an attempt to combine popular attributes of diverse breeds with dissimilar gaits and/or conformation to produce a desirable new look for the marketplace.

While the first cross of these differing breeds is sometimes popular, bringing a higher-than-expected price for uniqueness, the resultant gene pool is often unpredictable for future breeding generations. When mixing gene pools of dissimilar breeds, it is impossible to ascertain which characteristics of each breed will express itself in future offspring. For example, an Arabian bred to a Clydesdale in the hope of creating an elegant powerhouse sport horse may, in reality, result in a squat, full-bodied horse with tiny hooves, a Roman head, camped-out hindquarters and a fiery temperament. One can only guess the direction of future breedings. Often, these crosses result in a very disappointing end to an enthusiastic dream.

Ultimately, the most reliable parentage choices are individuals with long-proven gene pools that are best suited physically and mentally for the discipline in which their offspring will perform. When considering the strengths of a stallion and a mare, research each individual's genotype (genetic constitution) and phenotype (physical characteristics as determined by its genotype).

Stallions with strong phenotypic traits are said to stamp their foals. They can particularly improve a mare that is genetically ineffectual. In this scenario, the mare genetically loses herself, becoming a vessel for the stallion while her foal assumes a majority of the stallion's characteristics. On the other hand, a stallion who lacks strong phenotypic traits will only pass on genotype, resulting in dissimilar characteristics with his offspring. Taken from the other side, a mare who is genetically prepotent can prevent a stallion from overriding her type in her offspring.

How much of what you see in a horse is the result of its raising and handling (nurture) versus its genetic basis (nature)? Conventional wisdom would have us believe that breeding is a 50/50 proposition with both parents contributing half the genetic material. In reality the mare may have a slightly greater influence on the end product due to her constant daily contact and her temperament that will have a direct affect on the foal's relationships with other horses and people.

Therefore, it is imperative to choose the best broodmare candidate for your financial circumstances. There are four main options in selecting your future broodmare:

1. Breed the existing mare in your barn. If you have elected to breed the mare you currently own, the only choice you have in the breeding equation is the selection of the stallion. Your mare enters the breeding experience as-is with no opportunity for personal genetic improvement or alteration.

Is your mare registered or grade? If she is registered, is she currently accepted in an approved studbook that is compatible with the stallion you wish to use? If not, is she qualified to participate in breed inspections of the chosen stallion's registry in the hope of receiving inspection scores to make her eligible for inclusion in his studbook?

To avoid disappointment, your mare should be presented at an inspection *before* breeding. Do not accept the stallion owner's assurance that acceptance as a breeding mare into his stallion's breed registry is a mere formality. Certain warmblood registries have extremely strict evaluation criteria for mares outside the breed, often requiring higher inspection scores of the outside applicant than from purebred mares. They may even refuse to inspect some outside mares or will assign evaluation scores too low for the mare to be accepted into the studbook. Presenting your mare at a breed registry inspection is not an inexpensive proposition. To avoid disappointment, realistically evaluate your mare's strengths, then select a registry for which you feel she meets the standard.

If your mare does not have papers or is of a type lacking in gaits or conformation to pass an inspection, her foal cannot be registered with most warmblood associations despite the sire's ranking or the quality of the foal. Breed registration papers are an important consideration as they will increase your foal's value and marketability, particularly if you are breeding for resale.

2. Purchase a mare specifically to suit your breeding goals. This option may give you a better opportunity to produce the type of foal you want. You can preselect the breed and bloodlines best suited to the creation of your ideal sport horse. The only limitation is your budget.

Your ideal candidate will be younger than ten years of age and will exhibit good physical condition. Research has proven that age and the previous number of foals will affect a mare's future fertility. If she has existing offspring, they will provide you with the opportunity to examine what she can produce. Do her foals appeal to you? Does she stamp them with her gaits, conformation and temperament?

Assess her rideability and temperament. Does she have a performance record? If so, was she ridden by a professional or handled by an amateur? If a mare has a difficult temperament, but still appeals to you because of physical type or athletic ability, research her bloodlines to ascertain whether she will be prone to pass on her temperament.

Is she registered with a breed association? What scores did she receive from the judges at her inspection for body type and gaits? Has she been awarded any distinctions within her registry? If she has offspring, how have they scored at their inspections? Does she come from a strong mare line? Certain mare lines can be traced for positive heritable traits which are passed from mare to filly that should be evident in the next generation regardless of the choice of stallion.

A cost-saving option is to purchase a young filly who is representative of the breed, bloodlines and physical type that you wish to reproduce. The "buy now/breed later" plan offers delayed gratification for people who want to breed quality horses but do not have the budget to purchase a top-quality, established mare. Time, space and patience for the filly to grow are necessary parts of this equation.

3. Lease a mare. This option can give you access to a better mare than you might be able to afford in an outright purchase. This short-term option gives you the opportunity to vary your breeding program from season to season by switching mares and introducing different bloodlines to your breeding plan each year.

There is no established protocol for leasing. Be sure your contract is very specific on points of responsibility and liability. For example, do you pay the owner board to keep the leased mare at her farm, or can you move the mare to a farm of your choosing for the duration of the pregnancy? Lease-mare owners frequently wish to retain management control of their horses. While the end result will hopefully be the foal of your dreams, you will miss the hands-on aspects of the breeding experience if the mare remains with her owner.

Your contract should also address equine liability insurance. If you insure the lease mare, how is her value determined and what is covered? If major decisions such as surgery or euthanasia need to be made during the term of the contract, who is responsible to make them, and who bears the financial burden? As with any contractual matter, you may want to consult a lawyer with experience in equine law.

Expenses can easily escalate in a leasing program, especially if the mare does not become pregnant in the first season. For example, you have a nonrefundable stallion contract with a live foal guarantee, but the lease mare did not catch during the contracted breeding season. Do you cross your fingers and renew the lease for a second year? Or do you walk away with no foal as well as being out the stud fee, lease fee and mare care fees? This is a big, costly decision! Be sure your contract covers a variety of scenarios.

4. Utilize embryo transfer. This final breeding option is a very expensive and complicated proposition. It will require you to have one mare as an embryo donor plus a second mare to serve as the embryo recipient. Reasons to consider embryo transfer include owning a valuable mare who cannot carry a foal to term, an actively competitive mare who is not at a point in her career to take a "foal break," or a mare whose health or that of her fetus may be jeopardized by a full term pregnancy.

The process of embryo transfer requires that ovulation must be synchronized between the donor and recipient mares. Once your mare has been bred, the veterinarian will collect her 6-day-old fertilized embryo. The embryo is then implanted in the recipient mare who carries it to term. The odds for success are low with an overall pregnancy rate of only 25–50 percent per cycle. Problems with the fertility of either of the mares or of the stallion, difficulty in synchronizing the cycles of the mares or inexperienced veterinary personnel will result in a disappointingly lower success rate.

If you are considering this method of reproduction, be sure to check if it is accepted by your chosen breed association. Some registries do not recognize embryo transfer or have restrictions regarding the number of registered foals one mare may produce in a given year.

Before you have finalized your choice of mare candidate, it is important to have your veterinarian conduct a breeding soundness examination (BSE). This exam will determine if your mare is a physically suitable candidate for breeding. It assesses her reproductive health rather than her athletic ability or conformation. It will answer the important questions of whether or not she can conceive, carry to term and deliver a live, healthy foal. Spending a little money up front with your veterinarian to confirm healthy reproductive functions in the mare prior to contracting with a stallion will save you time, money and stress in the long run.

The BSE will begin externally with an evaluation of the mare's vulvar conformation to determine how well the edges of the vulva meet to create a "seal" against bacteria and outside air. Mares with a tipped vulva resulting in a sunken rectum can have difficulties maintaining a pregnancy. A poor vulva angle can result in the accumulation of stool, urine and/or air, causing contamination and a hostile environment in the uterus. Age and body fat can affect the appearance of vulvar conformation. Older and/or underweight mares may have a sunken appearance to the rectum and upper portion of the vulvar opening.

If your mare exhibits less-than-ideal vulvar conformation, you will want to consider a Caslick procedure. This procedure will require your veterinarian to suture together the edges of the top portion of the mare's vulva, leaving the lower portion open to permit urination. The upper lips of the vulva heal together, creating a barrier against fecal contamination and air sucking. The Caslick sutures will need to be removed a month prior to foaling to prevent tearing by the foal during delivery. After foaling, the vulva should be resutured to prevent future contamination.

Next on the exam will be an internal vaginal exam to confirm that urine is not pooling in the vagina, a serious condition that interferes with uterine health. Your veterinarian then verifies that the mare's cervix is intact and capable of closing sufficiently to maintain a pregnancy. A uterine culture should be run at this time to check for evidence of a bacterial or yeast infection.

Your veterinarian should also do an ultrasound to ascertain that the mare possesses two healthy ovaries. He will also check for the presence of fluid or cysts inside the uterus. The ultrasound also can confirm the results of a positive uterine culture. If there is no fluid present in the ultrasound, the cause of the positive reading is probably just fecal contamination which does not require treatment.

The ultrasound can also detect endometrial cysts that may develop in older mares who have produced numerous foals. Your veterinarian should note and chart the location of any cysts if present. Cysts can negatively impact the fertility of the mare by hindering embryonic development in its migration phase. If not identified prior to breeding, they may be mistaken for a pregnancy on an ultrasound check which can cause incorrect assumptions about the mare's reproductive status.

Another area to consider on the BSE is a uterine biopsy. This procedure is strongly advised for nonmaiden mares as well as for older maiden mares. The biopsy results will tell you the statistical likelihood that the mare's uterus can maintain a pregnancy due to existing scar tissue, inflammation or infection from a previous pregnancy. A uterus is graded on a scale of 1A, for ideal, to a 3—essentially no chance of sustaining a pregnancy. The grade can improve with treatment for an active infection. If you have an exceptional performance mare with outstanding bloodlines who has an unacceptable uterine biopsy, she may be a candidate for embryo transfer.

The ideal conclusion for your mare's BSE is a negative culture, no fluid or cysts present on the ultrasound, a 1A uterine biopsy, two ovaries with normal appearance, a rectal exam that rules out any fistulas or tears, and good vulvar conformation.

Nonmaiden mares should also have a basic broodmare health history, including previous foaling date, cycling patterns and any reproductive tract abnormalities. How many foals has she produced? Date of last breeding? Date of last foaling? Does she have a history of genital infection? What is her typical length of gestation? Does she tend to twin? Did she have any difficulties foaling? Does she produce sufficient milk? Is she a good, nurturing mother? This is important information to know as you prepare to breed.

Personal Journey

From the beginning, I was confident in my selection of Anastasia as a broodmare prospect. Purchasing her as a weanling had given me three valuable years prior to breeding to truly assess her qualities. Beyond her top-flight bloodlines and conformation that had motivated me to purchase her, I grew continually impressed with her temperament and trainability as we worked during her early years.

Always keenly alert, she also possessed a logical side that made her more apt to take exploratory steps toward an unknown rather than to flee in panic mode. From focused obedience showing in-hand to willing acceptance of a saddle, bridle and rider, she rarely disappointed and was an enjoyable partner in the training process.

The big unknowns were the strength of her phenotype and her maiden mare status. Being a youngster herself, she had no established history of how much of herself she would pass on to her offspring. However, I knew from the experience of owning two Edinburg progeny that he was very prepotent, passing on his conformation and gaits to both of my horses and others I had seen.

Although Anastasia and my gelding, Horizon, were from different dams, their physical resemblance was uncanny. They both possessed the same striking chiseled head and elegant topline. At first glance, there was no mistaking their direct relationship. However, despite all this physical evidence, it would remain a mystery until foaling day whether or not Anastasia would have the phenotype to continue the Edinburg tradition by passing her desirable traits on to her newborn.

In addition to appearance and temperament, there was an equally important question of Anastasia's acceptance of motherhood. Would she be a good, nurturing mother? Would she instinctively love and accept her foal? Or would she reject it, refusing to let it nurse even to the point of aggressive behavior? With no track record, there was no way to answer this great unknown until the moment arrived.

Dr. Strosnider arrived at my farm in mid-January, 2003 to conduct a breeding soundness exam on Anastasia. Although I did not plan to breed her until mid-April, we wanted to check her out early in the season in case there were any infections or other problems that required treatment. Happily, Anastasia received a clean bill of breeding soundness with a negative culture, no fluid or cysts, two normal ovaries and good vulvar conformation that would not require a Caslick.

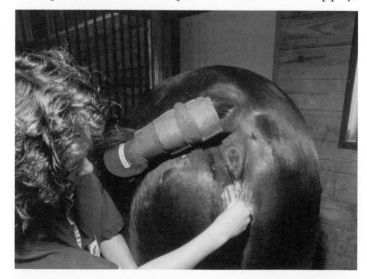

Vet tech assistant Jenny Bruns thoroughly cleans Anastasia in preparation for her breeding soundness exam.

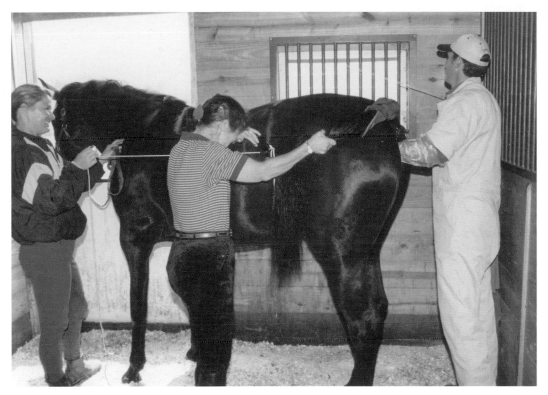

It was a team effort by my good friend Leslie Crombie and me to assist Dr. Strosnider during his rectal palpation of Anastasia on the breeding soundness exam.

I gave Anastasia a long, thoughtful pat when we received the good news. It looked like the time, conditions and the stars were aligning for us to start down the road for which we had been preparing for the past three years.

Chapter 4

The "It" Factor

Now that you have made the decision on a mare to breed and are satisfied that she fulfills your broodmare requirements, it's time to turn your attention to the other half of the breeding equation and consider the stallion candidates. It's important to note that in the grand financial plan of breeding your mare, the cost of the stud fee is minimal. A major perk for sport horse breeders today is the accessibility and affordability of top stallions throughout the world. Modern technology offers mare owners access to a virtual smorgasbord of the best bloodlines.

In general, the financial difference between accessing a mediocre or unproven sport horse stallion and the absolute best of a breed is a mere fraction of the total investment in the production of your foal. Therefore, the price of the stud fee should not be a determinant in your choice of stallion. If you cannot afford the stud fee, you cannot afford to breed a quality sport horse.

The majority of mare owners have their first contact with a stallion on the pages of the voluminous breeding issues that are published by major equine magazines each winter. The mare owner is barraged by hundreds of glossy ads representing every sport horse possibility, from the obscure to highly popular, all promising the genes that will produce the biggest, the best and the brightest that your imagination and mare can conjure.

Page after page of enticing information bombards mare owners. Some ads are amateurish home computer presentations, but more and more are the slick creations of top quality advertising agencies, designed with the same attention to lighting, composition and copy as top fashion magazine ads. And the similarities do not end there.

The product they are selling is often the same—sex. They market both the chemistry and look of their product to grab you with the *"it"* factor. The goal is to elicit the "I've got to have it" reaction from you, the prospective buyer. Clever marketing can enhance even a mediocre horse, but given the right photographic layout and enticing copy, that special stallion will leap right off the page with a captivating charisma that gives you goose bumps.

A special ad grabs you. The image on the page more than fulfills the expectations that you have been holding up as the standard in your search. You are positive that you are in love with the look and achievements of this stallion. There is no need to look any further. But wait! Don't fall head over heels until you do your homework.

Make sure this is really the "man" you want to bring home to your mare. Remember that advertising often can be deceptive. Don't let a terrific photo and creative copy supersede your ultimate goal. There is a lot more research to be done beyond thumbing through the pages of a magazine. Stick to your evaluation criteria with the appealing ad as confirmation of your ultimate selection.

To avoid being overwhelmed by the number of potential stallions, begin your selection process by narrowing the breed choices to those that are compatible with your mare. If she has been approved by a breed registry, the choice of stallion breed is obvious if your goal is to produce a registered foal. Due to desirable type, performance and progeny, some stallions are approved by multiple registries, making them available to a wider cross section of mares. If your mare has not been approved, you are not locked into a specific breed choice.

Unless you have a specific stallion in mind, the available options can be overwhelming even when you have narrowed the breed type. You may find yourself overloaded with advice from friends, experts and advertisements. Who do you trust to give you the best information?

If you plan to attend a breed inspection with your mare, the judging jury is an excellent source of advice to help match your mare with an appropriate stallion. They have firsthand knowledge of your mare's bloodlines as well as the available stallions that would cross well. Another popular source of information is online breeding forums. However, they may frequently be misleading or slanted depending on who is doing the talking. And then there are the individual stallion owners who may also tend to be biased toward their horse or representatives of his bloodlines.

Accurate data on every approved stallion is available if you are willing to do the research. Warmblood registries in the United States and Europe publish annual stallion directories. This valuable source of information includes pedigrees, stallion inspection scores, competition results, offspring information, breeder contacts and photos. The directories can be obtained by directly contacting the respective registries.

The Web sites of the various national sport horse organizations are another excellent source for stallion information, offering performance results for sires and their offspring as well as pedigree data. Depending on your discipline, the following Web sites are good places to start:

United States Equestrian Federation (www.usef.org)
United States Dressage Federation (www.usdf.org)
International Hunter Futurity (www.inthf.org)
International Jumper Futurity (www.youngjumpers.com)
United States Eventing Association (www.eventingusa.com)
World Breeding Federation for Sport Horses (www.wbfsh.com)

Online auctions are gaining in popularity as an option for mare owners who are looking for discounted stud fees. The proceeds of the auctions benefit the host association because the stud fees are generously donated by stallion owners. Not all auctions are breed based: some auctions may are held by performance organizations.

Choose the auction that best suits you and your mare based on breed or performance preference. If bidding for a specific breed, be sure your mare is approved so her foal can be registered with the association.

In most cases, your winning bid will only include the stud fee. Although each stallion auction contract may differ, the mare owner is usually responsible for the additional cost of booking, shipping and collection fees. Before placing a bid, check with the stallion owner regarding the breed-back policy if your mare does not become pregnant on the first try as well as the live-foal guarantee. Based on the answers to your questions, you may discover that the auction price is not really a discount. In many cases, it may be more cost-effective to pay the full stud fee in order to gain the full benefits. For a more detailed discussion of these policies, see page 43.

Once you have narrowed your list, another good source of information is promotional videotapes. While the video should not be your final determinant, it can help eliminate a lot of maybes. If correctly composed, the video should present a sample of progeny as well as the stallion himself. As in magazine ads, the quality of videos varies greatly from backyard handicams to professional productions choreographed to music. Always keep in mind that clever video editing can hide faults as well as enhance strengths.

If your budget allows, arrange a visit to your short-listed stallions at their home farms or competitions. Nothing can compare to watching the stallion perform right in front of you, with all his plusses, minuses and character on display.

Visiting a stallion in person gives you the opportunity to meet his progeny. Ultimately, what he produces is more important to you than the stallion himself as you are not investing directly in him but in the genes he passes on.

Hopefully the breeding farm will also have representative offspring of various ages so you can compare them at different stages of development. Pretty in the field and functional in the competition arena are not always one and the same. Have they attended an inspection? If so, how do their inspection scores compare with their sire's scores as well as their siblings? If they have been shown, gather information on their performance record showing in-hand as well as under saddle.

Does the stallion stamp his offspring with his look and movement? Study the youngsters' physical strengths and weaknesses. For example, is the stallion's bloodline known for extravagant gaits and trainability? Does the bloodline have a predisposition for conformational weaknesses such as long backs, short necks or sickle hocks, or more serious defects such as parrot mouth, or a tendency to develop osteochondrosis dessicans? If some, but not all, show weaknesses, try to examine their dams before putting all of the blame on the stallion, because some mares may genetically override the stallion.

If color is important to you, inquire about the percentage of foals thrown with your desired color. Discuss with the stallion owner and your veterinarian the likelihood that your mare will produce a desired color when bred to this stallion. Also address the question of whether a particular color selection will result in a healthy foal, because some color genes are incompatible and may be lethal to the foal. For example, breeding a Paint overo mare to a Paint overo stallion can lead to a fatal gastrointestinal birth defect called lethal white syndrome.

Data gathering is relatively easy to do with a proven stallion whose performance results and offspring are public record. In your quest, also try to contact current owners or riders of offspring from your stallion of interest. They can give you firsthand input regarding the temperament, athleticism and trainability they have experienced with the offspring. Another good place to study the stallion's progeny is in the competition ring in classes designed specifically to showcase young talent. In-hand breed classes at recognized dressage or hunter shows are a great way to compare young horses. For the more advanced youngsters, the International Hunter Futurity and the International Jumper Futurity offer over-fences championships. Top 4-, 5- and 6-year-old dressage horses compete in the FEI Young Horse Championships.

However, your research becomes much more difficult with a young, unproven stallion with no offspring of competition age. The best way to assess a young stallion prospect is through stallion evaluation inspection scores, personal show records and bloodlines, particularly his mare line in the German breeds.

When stallions and mares are evaluated at an official breed association kuering, they receive bonit scores from the judging panel. These scores range from 1-10 and are assigned to various parts of the horse's body as well as the gaits. Bonit scores become an integral part of a registered horse's permanent record.

If your mare has been inspected, comparing her bonit scores with the prospective stallion's scores will help you select a horse best suited to improve her weaknesses. Look for areas where he can best enhance her. For example, your mare only scored a 6 for her trot, but your stallion candidate scored a 9. This stallion is potentially a good choice to improve her gaits. However, always keep in mind that parents possessing traits on opposite ends of the scoring spectrum do not guarantee a foal that meets them in the middle.

Study bloodlines for the strengths you want to reproduce in your foal. Despite comparable attributes, not all stallions are equal in the athletic ability they pass on to their offspring. Some bloodlines are known for superior jumping skills, while others excel in the ability to collect for upper level dressage. Don't be fooled by a pretty face. Do your homework!

The German breed associations called Verbands track the mare lines as carefully as the stallion lines by attaching a *stamm* number behind the mare's name to identify her mare line. A *stamm* can be compared to a route like a vine that twines through the mare line. Mares pass this number on to their offspring who keep it on their papers for identification. Certain *stamm* lines are very famous for producing upper level performance horses. A particularly successful Holsteiner line is 162. This line was represented by 4 horses competing in show jumping in the 2004 Olympics.

Before you sign a contract, be sure to ascertain the stallion's fertility. There are three important questions you should address with the stallion's owner: 1. How many mares did he breed last year? 2. How many mares did he get pregnant last year? and 3. How many mares became pregnant on the first breeding attempt?

No matter how phenomenal your stallion choice looks and performs, if the quality of his semen is poor, you may want to consider another candidate. When evaluating for artificial insemination with fresh-cooled semen, you will need to consider the sperm motility and longevity for up to 48 hours. The higher the motility the better. Each insemination dose at collection should contain approximately 500 million live sperm. Be aware that the motility percentage at collection will drop by as much as 50 percent within the 24-hour or longer shipping cycle when you hope to breed your mare. Be sure to ask the stallion owner for motility percentages at collection, as well as at 24- and 48-hours after collection to allow for time lost in shipment.

The percentage of motility is greatly affected by the person who reads it. Be sure your veterinarian allows the semen to warm to room temperature when it is removed from the transport container. If on removal from the container, the semen is immediately put on a cool or cold slide for checking under a microscope, you will get a false reading as it will not be motile.

There also should be a morphologic evaluation to ascertain the number of normally shaped sperm. Sperm must have a specific shape in order to successfully impregnate the egg. Fertility will drop with a high number of abnormally shaped sperm.

When all the pieces fall into place and you finally decide on the stallion who promises to be the ideal match for your mare, it is a relief to put the research, questioning and soul searching behind. Now it is time to get on with the job of creating your dream foal.

But wait! There still remain the details of the stallion contract. Put the love of the stallion aside until you familiarize yourself with the ramifications of his contract. Since you are about to sign a legally binding document to seal your relationship with the stallion's owner for the next year or longer, it may be a good idea to consult with an attorney who is familiar with horse-breeding practices. Read the wording carefully to understand exactly what you are signing. It is hard for the novice breeder to grasp how many things can go wrong in the course of creating a foal. Be certain your contract covers you for those eventualities.

Ask the stallion owner the following questions before you sign on the dotted line:

1. Is there a live foal guarantee? The normally accepted definition of live foal guarantee is that the foal stands and nurses for a 24-hour period after birth. If the foal does not survive this period, you should receive breed-back privileges to the stallion without having to pay an additional stud fee. However, you will still be responsible for paying all future collection and shipping fees as well as the possibility of another booking fee. See page 45 for more on this.

Be certain you clearly understand the stallion owner's definition of live foal guarantee as written in your contract because there may be various interpretations. The contract should explicitly outline how long the stallion owner will honor the live foal guarantee, as well as if it is transferable to another mare should complications arise with your original contract mare or the contract stallion.

2. What is the stallion's breeding season? Do not assume that the stallion's breeding season will extend indefinitely. Many stallions have cutoff dates for what their owners feel is the appropriate end of the season. Familiarize yourself with the stallion's availability during the breeding season. Some stallions also have restricted breeding schedules dictated by competition demands.

Due to the popularity of a stallion, some owners will refuse to accept contracts that exceed the appropriate number of mares they feel their operation or stallion can handle. This limitation policy usually does not apply when frozen semen is requested due to the constant availability of frozen semen until all straws are depleted.

3. Can my breeding rights be transferred to a replacement mare should my original mare become incapacitated? Although this thought is far from your mind as you happily dream of breeding your treasured mare to this special stallion, circumstances beyond your control can and do occur. Before you achieve a full-term foal, the contract mare may prove infertile, she may be sold, your lease on her may expire or she may die. Be sure your contract is not nullified in the event of any of these occurrences.

4. Is there a stallion substitution policy? If the contract stallion becomes unbreedable due to infertility, sale or death, how will the contract be honored? Frequently, when a stallion is sold, the new owner does not assume responsibility for the existing contracts or honor the old owner's obligations to contracted mare owners. Your contract to a specific stallion may become invalid with his sale. If your mare did not become pregnant, you may have no recourse to rebreed. Be sure to include a clause in your contract specifying acceptable alternatives, in the event that a sale may occur.

Many stallion owners stand multiple stallions. They may reserve the right in your contract to utilize a substitute stallion should the originally contracted stallion become incapacitated. Beware that the substitute stallion may not be approved by the same association as the contract stallion, causing a dilemma when it comes to registering your foal. In another scenario, the substitute stallion may only be available through frozen semen, but not all mares can be bred with frozen semen. If you are uncomfortable with the contractual clause allowing stallion switching, be sure to make the appropriate alterations prior to signing.

5. What is the stallion's collection schedule? Collection schedules vary from farm to farm. The standard schedule is Monday, Wednesday and Friday, but some stallion owners are flexible and willing to work with your mare's specific needs. It is important to try to cycle your mare to fit the stallion's collection schedule. Another complication to your timetable is the shipping schedule of airfreight carriers that will not ship or deliver on Sundays or may be delayed or rerouted by inclement weather.

Most stallion owners require advance notification by the mare owner when the semen will be needed. Notification may be required as far as a week in advance. This type of time constraint may prove to be very difficult when trying to regulate a mare's cycle. Good luck guesstimating your mare's ideal breeding day a week out!

6. If breeding to a private-treaty stallion, what are his specific requirements? Private-treaty is a non-published breeding agreement individualized to each specific mare. The requirements will vary from stallion to stallion. Some of the many reasons owners stand a private-treaty stallion are: 1. The owner is not highly motivated to breed an actively competing horse. Private-treaty allows him to pick and choose his mares, possibly giving a successful show mare a discounted rate while charging an exorbitant stud fee to an unknown mare. 2. Private-treaty serves as a reputation protector for the young stallion to prevent him from taking on too many poor-to-mediocre quality mares. 3. Private-treaty can be used to entice the owners of the best mare candidates to inquire on the chance they may get a deal. 4. Private-treaty is a way to avoid publishing a stud fee until the stallion owner ascertains the type of mares with which they will be dealing.

7. What fees will I incur beyond the stud fee? Do not assume that the published stud fee is the only service cost you will incur in your contract. Additional standard services include booking fees, collection fees, shipping fees and container deposits, all of which are individually determined by the stallion owner.

Booking fees refer to the time and paperwork required by the stallion owner to authenticate the contract between the mare and the stallion. This is usually a nonrefundable fee. For example, if your mare is unable to conceive and you do not have a replacement mare, the stud fee may possibly be refunded, but not the booking fee. In another scenario, if your mare is unable to produce a live foal and you invoke the contract's live foal guarantee to breed your mare back the following season, you may not be responsible for a second stud fee. However, you probably will have to pay a second booking fee due to the additional paperwork.

Collection fees can vary widely from breeding farm to breeding farm. For example, stallion "A" may cost $125 per collection while stallion "B" costs $400 per collection. Why does it cost so much more to do basically the same function? Stallion owners who do their own on-site collection, lab work, packaging and shipping can control their costs and frequently pass on these savings. On the other hand, stallions that must be collected by outside specialty services will incur greater expenses that the stallion owner must pass on to mare owners.

The stallion owner will supply a specially designed semen shipping container. You will be expected to pay a container deposit fee at the start of the breeding process. This is a one-time, up-front charge that is traditionally refunded at the end of the breeding season or when you return the container after your final usage. This fee varies: containers for frozen semen are the most expensive.

All container shipping fees from the stallion to your mare and back to the breeding farm are your responsibility. Shipments are generally done by overnight airfreight with a rapid turnaround of the container back to the stallion owner as soon as you have removed the product. These containers are expensive and much-used during the breeding season, so mare owners are frequently assessed a fine for delayed returns.

The final fact to confirm before signing the contract is that your chosen stallion has been licensed to breed by his respective association. Individual performance, offspring performance and fertility rates may result in different levels of licensing within the registry. Just because a stallion possesses personal papers from a breed registry does not automatically mean that he has been inspected and approved for breeding by that registry. You should check directly with the registry office for confirmation of the current status of your chosen stallion's breeding license.

Feel free to ask questions of the stallion owner and expect clear answers. This is a person with whom you will have a long-term relationship, often conducted entirely long distance via telephone or e-mail. The stallion owner plays a major role in the ease or difficulty in which your foal is conceived. If you understand and agree with the terms of the breeding farm's contract, and have faith in the product, it is time to sign on the dotted line.

Personal Journey

Having purchased Anastasia as a weanling, I had the luxury of several years to ponder the selection of her ideal cross. While I was delighted with the elegance and trainability of my mare, the ultimate challenge for the breeder is to improve on the parents. With that in mind, I focused my search for a stallion who would free Anastasia's shoulders and add scope to her gaits, especially her canter.

Although the ability to access the worldwide pool of Swedish Warmblood stallions was tempting, I decided for my first breeding experience it would be best to utilize fresh-cooled semen from a stateside stallion. Anastasia and I would face enough challenges in our first breeding attempt without the added complication and cost presented by using frozen semen from a European stallion. Importing fresh-cooled semen from Europe was not an option due to the time needed for collection, shipping and delivery.

Another consideration was that my farm vet was proficient in the techniques of artificial insemination utilizing fresh-cooled semen. However, the use of frozen semen would have necessitated a higher level of technology than could have been confidently implemented at my farm. For the best chance of success utilizing frozen semen would have required cycling Anastasia then trailering her to a theriogenologist's clinic when she was ready to be bred. The closest recommended specialist was a three-hour drive from my farm. There were just too many complications that made the use of frozen semen an unnecessary piece in an already complicated puzzle. Maybe next time.

The decision of a stallion solved itself when Anastasia was still two years away from being bred. The well-known and highly successful breeding stallion, Vivaldi, who had been standing at stud in Sweden, was imported to the United States. He was currently standing at Three Crowns Farm in Woodinville, Washington.

A top-ranking producer in Sweden, Vivaldi's reputation in the United States was well established by his offspring who had been imported before him. I had personally admired several of his outstanding get who were competing successfully at the FEI levels. My friend and mentor, Major Anders Lindgren, with whom I had

Photo by Rik van Lent

A top sire of quality Swedish Warmbloods in Sweden and the U.S., Vivaldi possessed the ideal traits of conformation, movement and temperament to enhance Anastasia's qualities.

EVALUATION BY THE SWEDISH INSPECTION COMMITTEE: PREMIUM A

Conformation (scale 1 - 10)

Type: 9   Head, Neck, Body: 9   Legs: 8   Walk: 8   Trot: 10   Total: 44

Gaits under rider (scale 1 - 10):   Walk: 8   Trot: 10   Canter: 9

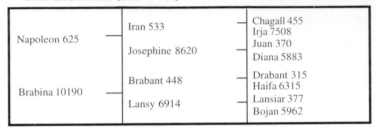

Vivaldi's pedigree in addition to his excellent stallion inspection evaluation promised to compliment Anastasia's bloodlines.

trained for many years, personally confirmed my selection of Vivaldi as the best prospect for Anastasia based on his lifetime of experience with Swedish Warmbloods and knowledge of bloodlines.

Vivaldi himself was trained to Grand Prix, exhibiting a strong talent for piaffe and passage. His success as a stallion had made him one of the highest ranked sires of dressage horses in Sweden, particularly known for producing superior gaits and conformation. As a young horse, he had won his stallion test, scoring on a 1–10 scale: Type: 9; Head, neck, body: 9; Legs: 8; Walk: 8; Trot: 10; and Gaits under rider: Walk: 8, Trot: 10, Canter: 9.

My only hesitation regarding selecting Vivaldi was his age. At the time of the planned breeding to Anastasia, he would be 19. Several friends who were respected breeders questioned the fertility of such a senior stallion. While they suggested it might not be as much of an issue if we were breeding on site with immediate access to insemination on collection, the time required to ship the semen would lower motility. If a senior stallion's motility diminished with age, would it not be even further decreased after shipment, thus affecting the ability to successfully impregnate my mare?

Vivaldi's owner assured me that her stallion was still highly fertile with a motility rate 24 hours after collection averaging 70 percent. For shipped, fresh-cooled semen the previous season, 23 out of 29 mares bred by Vivaldi became pregnant, a 79 percent average. The math on paper was convincing enough to proceed.

The Three Crowns Farm contract was straightforward: a non-refundable booking fee was due on signing. Half of the breeding fee was due when my mare was confirmed pregnant by ultrasound 21 days after breeding. The balance of the breeding fee was not due until the foal was a week old.

If my mare failed to conceive within the contracted breeding season, I would not be responsible for the balance of the breeding fee. However, no pregnancy meant no breed-back rights. If my mare did conceive but reabsorbed during the term of the pregnancy or gave birth to a foal who died within the first week of life, I would have the right to rebreed in the following season. In either case, my veterinarian was required to confirm in writing to the stallion owner my mare's status at each contracted stage.

The live foal guarantee was the catch in my contract. It could only be activated if my mare conceived in the first place. If we failed to get her pregnant, I would forfeit half the breeding fee as well as the booking fee.

The first collection and shipping fees were included in the booking fee. However, any additional shipping and collection fees were to be my responsibility, payable at the time of the service. Three Crowns Farm requested that semen be ordered for collection prior to 10 a.m. Pacific time on a Monday, Wednesday or Friday, the day before it would be needed. However, they assured me they would attempt to work with my mare's specific needs if her cycle differed from their collection schedule.

On March 21, 2003, I mailed a copy of Anastasia's papers, a signed contract and the $500 booking fee to Three Crowns Farm. I had officially set the wheels in motion, confident in my choice of Vivaldi and his team who would be an important part of the process over the next year.

Chapter 5

Preparing the Mare and Yourself

Breeding is not an art. Do not approach the experience of breeding your mare as a mystic rite of nature that seeks to align the stages of fertility and, with luck, produce a foal. Rather, viewed from a logical perspective, breeding is a science. When you implement the science correctly, the result—barring unforeseen circumstances—is usually a pregnancy. Make it your objective to learn the basic tenets of the science before you and your mare begin the process. Knowledge will help to make your breeding experience efficient, which equals savings in dollars and time.

As you prepare to breed your mare, this is the time to educate yourself regarding what to do, when to do it, and who to ask if you are not sure. The breeding season is not a time for trial and error or finger crossing. Your working relationship with the veterinarian who will breed your mare will be enhanced in direct proportion to the amount of knowledge you bring into the process. Beyond reading and talking with experienced horse breeders, you may also want to consider taking a short course in breeding if available through your local university or extension service.

Nature has a grand reproduction plan for all her creatures. We need to be cognizant of the bylaws of the plan as they apply to our horses. Learn how to recognize the signs of your mare's heat cycle to ascertain what she is doing hormonally. As she settles into estrous, she will do specific things at specific times. Your job is to recognize and chart that behavior prior to breeding. Doing a thorough job on your reproductive homework will return dividends in the long run.

Mares are seasonally polyestrous breeders with a reproductive and nonreproductive season. During their breeding season they will exhibit several estrous or "heat" cycles. The length of natural daylight regulates their repro-ductive cycles. If your mare controlled her own breeding destiny, her biologi-cal clock would not permit her to cycle and breed with a resultant winter foal-ing. In the wild, the odds are stacked against winter offspring surviving the cold and lack of forage.

The majority of mares are anestrous—or nonreproductive—during the late fall and winter due to the lack of light. During the anestrous period, the mare's reproductive cycle takes a break, causing her to become sexually indifferent. Most mares usually stop exhibiting heat cycles during this time as their ovaries shrink in size and become inactive.

Between February and April, when the days begin to lengthen with increased daylight, mares enter the "transition period." This period also repeats in the fall as light diminishes and days are shortened. Although the mare may exhibit heat cycles, she may not experience normal ovulation. During this time, her reproductive functions are erratic as she slowly comes out of or returns to winter sexual hibernation. This may be reflected in inconsistent behavior and hormones, resulting in mixed signals and reproductive inefficiency. Because of the mixed physical signals emitted by the mare, recognizing the starting up or shutting down of her sexual systems can be a confusing time for the hopeful breeder.

In spring, the mare passes out of the "transition period" into estrous, her reproductive season. She is most fertile in May, June and July as the length of days and temperature increase. The mare usually achieves peak fertility on June 24, which is the longest day of the year.

Mare owners who decide to buck nature's natural order and breed for an early foal should realize that jumping the biological clock does not result in any physical benefit for the mare or foal. Depending on your geographic loca-tion, an early-season foal runs the risk of being born into a potentially hostile environment for climate and forage. From a financial investment standpoint, early breedings tend to be reproductively inefficient, as it is very hard to under-stand and manipulate the mare's cycle when Nature dictates that she should be anestrus.

As there is no physical benefit for the mare and foal, those who plan on early breeding usually have a purely competitive or monetary focus. The result-ing early foal will be bigger and stronger than most of his peers, giving him a leg up on the early-season competitions as well as meeting consumer demand for a well-developed, more mature young horse in the eyes of the judges and potential buyers. This is a serious consideration with the current interest in sport horse performance futurities. However, in the long run, genetics will determine the ultimate size of the adult horse.

Another reason to manipulate the mare's estrous cycle for an early- season breeding is to gain valuable extra time if you are planning a more involved method of breeding such as frozen semen or embryo transfer. You also may want to start early if you have a problem mare who requires additional time to get her hormones stabilized. Early breeding is also a consideration if you are planning to breed back your mare after foaling and do not want a late foal the following year.

Finally, if you do plan to breed early, be sure that your stallion of choice is available. Although stallions do not have a sexual season and can breed all year, most stallion owners restrict their horses' books to a specific season due to convenience and cost efficiency.

If you choose early breeding, you will need to use photo stimulation, the use of artificial lighting to push your mare into early cycling. Discuss with your veterinarian the method that is best suited for your specific situation.

A typical photo stimulation protocol begins 60 - 80 days prior to the desired breeding date by slowly increasing your mare's exposure to light. Beginning in October or November, increase the amount of light by 15 minutes per day until she receives 16 hours of light daily. Use a 200-watt clear bulb in the middle of a 12-foot by 12-foot stall, eliminating all shadows. Be sure both the light and fixture are fireproof. Do not deviate from the prescribed timetable. Leaving the lights on for a 24-hour period is not beneficial. Be aware that extreme cold can override the best-laid plans and the effect of artificial lighting. Current research suggests various methods of photostimulation. Discuss with your veterinarian the method that is best suited for your specific situation.

As you prepare to breed, learn to recognize the overt physical signs that your mare is in heat. Although behavior frequently varies from mare to mare, most exhibit a definite repetitive behavioral pattern. Pay attention to your mare. Keep a journal to help track her actions.

Astute cycle recognition will produce economic benefits. Depending on your chosen method of insemination, the highest pregnancy rates are achieved when ovulation occurs within 48 hours of breeding via live cover, 12 – 24 hours *before* ovulation utilizing artificial insemination with fresh-cooled semen, and less than six hours *after* ovulation with frozen semen.

Shipping and collection fees as well as veterinary service charges can rapidly escalate with every failed breeding attempt. In addition, if you have to rebreed numerous times because of misjudging your mare's cycle, there is an increased risk to the mare of uterine contamination due to additional examinations and reinseminations.

If your mare is stabled in a barn with other horses, see if there is a gelding to which she is attracted and willingly displays signs of heat. Some mares remain aloof to most gelding's advances, but may respond to the right horse with heightened interest. Other mares will only exhibit signs of heat for stallions or even a specific stallion that captures their attention.

Overt signs of heat may include provocative body language toward other horses such as raising her tail, squirting small amounts of urine and moving toward the teaser horse to squat and "wink" her vulva. A mare who is not in heat will exhibit the opposite behavior by moving away from the teaser, clamping her tail to her body, squealing or displaying aggressive actions such as pinning her ears, kicking or striking.

The mare's complete estrous cycle averages approximately 21–22 days. She is in estrus and receptive to breeding four to nine of these days. During the rest of the cycle, she is diestrus and not ovulating, thus incapable of becoming pregnant. Mares constantly produce follicles that are in various stages of maturation. As her cycle progresses, one follicle will become dominant. When the follicle is approximately 3–5 centimeters in size, it will ovulate, releasing the egg. The follicular cavity then collapses to form the corpus hemorrhagicum that fills with blood. This turns into the corpus luteum which is the structure that produces progesterone, the chemical responsible for maintaining pregnancy. If there is no resulting pregnancy from breeding, the CL regresses, prostaglandin is produced and the cycle repeats itself.

Although some people feel that Mother Nature knows best, understanding the function of specific hormones that can be administered to help "short cycle" or manipulate your mare's cycle often will take the guesswork out of when to breed to expedite a pregnancy. If the timing and technology is right, the cycle can be cut by as much as half. You can optimize your chances of conception through the use of hormones. These can be divided into two groups: cycle regulators (progesterone and prostaglandin) and ovulation inducers (human chorionic gonadotropin).

Progesterone can be used to establish a normal cycle in mares with follicular activity. It also can be used to maintain a pregnancy if it is believed that your mare does not produce sufficient amounts of progesterone on her own. The most commonly used is an orally administered synthetic progesterone analog called altrenogest (the brand name is Regumate, manufactured by Hoechst). Due to the reproductive-cycle-manipulating properties of this product, women should avoid bare-skin contact when administering it to their horses.

Prostaglandin can be used to short cycle a mare when her CL has produced sufficient amounts of progesterone to respond. This will cut down on the time between ovulation, and it will help you to better determine when your mare will ovulate. When administered, this injectable product may cause cramping, increased heart rate and sweating in the mare for a short time, usually less than an hour although it may seem longer to the concerned owner. A commonly used product is dinoprost tromethamine (the brand name is Lutalyse, manufactured by UpJohn).

Human chorionic gonadotropin helps to induce ovulation in a mare who is close to ovulating and exhibits a follicle of at least 3.5 centimeters. After injection of hCG, a large proportion of mares will ovulate within 12–48 hours. There is some controversy regarding the effectiveness of hCG with repeated usage within the same breeding season due to the mare developing antibodies to the product.

Deslorelin is a synthetic hormone given to induce ovulation in the mare. Use of the product results in an extremely high predictability of ovulation within 48 hours of insertion. Check with your veterinarian regarding distribution sources.

A simple recipe for a successful pregnancy early in the breeding season is to begin the mare on Regumate in the spring when you are preparing to breed. It should be given orally in your mare's feed for 10–14 days no matter where she is in her cycle. An average dose would equals 1cc per 110 pounds.

On the last day of administration, give the mare an intramuscular injection of prostaglandin. She will be ready to breed in about 5–10 days.

This formula makes it easier to expedite the collection and shipping of semen from the stallion owner. By knowing you will need the semen 7–10 days after administering the prostaglandin shot, you can coordinate the shipment to arrive approximately when your mare is ready to ovulate, eliminating much of the guesswork by having the semen available when you need it.

This recipe also works when rebreeding after foaling. Pregnancy rates on foal heat decrease since the mare's uterus needs some recovery time from giving birth. However, if you wish to breed your mare on her foal heat, start her on progesterone five days after foaling. Continue the Regumate for 10–14 days. On day 14, administer prostaglandin. Your mare can be ready to rebreed in 7–10 days, approximately 25 days after foaling. Using this system, you will maintain your calendar position without losing any time rebreeding. In the Perfect World scenario, your mare's initial pregnancy will run 340 days. Add 25 days to rebreed totaling 365 days in the breeding cycle.

Regumate is an excellent product for early season-breeding to help regulate your mare when she is coming out of the transitional stage. However, once the mare has begun to cycle regularly, her body may ignore the chemical affects of Regumate, resulting in frustration and loss of money for the breeder as unsuccessful attempt follows unsuccessful attempt to obtain a pregnancy.

An alternative to Regumate for controlling the mare's cycle is using daily injections of prostaglandin and estrogen. This protocol is particularly useful for breeders using frozen semen because it has a very high predictability in controlling the mare's cycle. Your veterinarian can guide you as to which technique will be the most efficient for you and your mare.

In addition to recognizing and managing your mare's cycling patterns, it is important to understand her changing nutritional requirements. Initially, the pregnant mare's dietary needs are similar to that of a non-pregnant mare. There is no formula diet for pregnancy. Each mare's needs should be individually considered relative to her environment and personal chemistry. Consult with your veterinarian, local extension service or feed dealer to get an accurate assessment of the nutritional value of the products you are currently feeding in your stable.

When developing a feeding program for your mare, realize that pregnancy rates are higher for average weight to fat mares than for those that are underweight. However, obesity should be avoided as it may result in a weak or undersized foal.

In early gestation (the period from conception through the sixth month), mares should be fed according to their level of exercise. Do not over-feed your horse just because she is pregnant. Note that by the sixth month of her pregnancy the fetus accounts for only two percent of the mare's total body weight. However, in late gestation (seven months to foaling), the now rapidly growing fetus' nutrient requirements will outpace the mare's maintenance requirements, necessitating changes in her dietary requirements for protein and minerals.

Too many people fall into the trap of overfeeding the pregnant mare into a state of obesity, while underfeeding the lactating mare when the stress on her personal dietary requirements is the greatest. The mare should gain weight in direct proportion to the growing fetus. Typically, a mare's weight should increase approximately 10–12 percent throughout the full term of her pregnancy, with the greatest gain in the final three months.

Good nutritional management of the pregnant mare should begin a year before you expect a foal on the ground. As with alterations to any feeding program, be sure to gradually phase in changes to prevent health issues. It is vital to fortify and protect your mare's personal store of vitamins and minerals that the growing fetus will deplete particularly in the final three months. Select a good quality broodmare supplement that includes the trace minerals iron, copper, zinc, manganese, calcium and phosphorus. You also should include vitamins A and E to compensate for limited grazing opportunities in the late months of gestation when winter weather conditions may restrict access to quality pasture. Discuss with your veterinarian the proper amounts to feed because fat-soluble vitamins can cause toxicity if ingested in excess.

To prevent mineral deficiency in the newborn, it is essential that the mare be supplemented throughout her pregnancy. Research indicates that a pri-mary cause of osteochondrosis dissecans (OCD) lesions in young horses is mineral deficiency. The fetus will draw heavily on the mare's mineral supplies in late gestation. The foal's initial mineral requirements will need to be met before birth because the mare's milk is not rich in minerals.

The developing fetus' growing demands for energy will increase the protein requirements of your mare throughout her pregnancy and beyond.

Mares require the most dietary energy in late gestation and during lactation. She will benefit from good quality hay and a grain or pelleted feed product of 14 percent protein. To help support the mare's increasing demands for calcium and protein, alfalfa may be gradually supplemented to reinforce a diet of grass hay or a pasture lacking in clover. Another source of palatable energy is fat supplementation via corn oil, vegetable oil or cocosoya which can increase calories without elevating carbohydrate levels.

Prior to beginning the breeding process, be sure your mare is current on her vaccinations. Immunization programs should be tailored to each individual mare depending on her history and the environment in which she resides. Mares that come into contact with outside horses through shows or a boarding barn environment will need additional protection. Barren mares should be vaccinated on their normal spring schedule, but prior to breeding because it is best to avoid any shots during the first trimester of pregnancy. All pregnant mares will require immunization against equine herpes virus type 1 which is one cause of abortion. This killed-virus vaccine should be administered in the fifth, seventh and ninth months.

Pregnant mares should receive boosters one month prior to foaling with basic coverage for tetanus, influenza, encephalomyelitis and West Nile. Be sure to check with your veterinarian since conditions in your specific area may dictate the need for additional vaccinations. While the broodmare will not transfer antibodies to her foal in utero, newborns will gain the vital disease-preventive antibodies through the mare's colostrum in the first hours of life.

Ascertain that your mare is parasite-free by running a baseline fecal exam. She should remain on a regular deworming program throughout her pregnancy. Before administering any wormer or medications, be sure to read the label for any cautions pertaining to pregnant or nursing mares.

Check her teeth and float if necessary. Since floating may require sedation, resolve any pressing dentistry issues prior to breeding as there may be risk involved to the embryo when sedating newly pregnant mares.

Finally, maintain regular farrier care throughout the pregnancy. Be sure your farrier has experience trimming broodmares. He will need to take into account the changing growth patterns that may result in flattened out "platter feet" caused by the increased weight of the foal in late gestation. It is suggested to pull all shoes prior to foaling unless your veterinarian or farrier recommends keeping them on the front due to the mare's individual needs.

Increased weight gain and decreased exercise and movement puts your pregnant mare at greater risk for developing laminitis. Be sure your farrier is on alert for any signs of hoof sole dropping or changes in the white line. For your part, regular manual checks for unusual hoof warmth or increased digital pulse are advised especially for mares with a previous history of laminitis. These symptoms in addition to abnormal discomfort in daily movement are cause to alert your veterinarian.

You have done your homework to familiarize yourself with your mare's reproductive behavior patterns. Her basic health and nutritional requirements have been fine-tuned. The regularity of her personal maintenance, combined with your newfound knowledge of the science of breeding, should provide confidence as you and your mare proceed to the next step in the process.

Personal Journey

When it came to equine reproduction, I was definitely a neophyte, so in the preparatory months, I dedicated myself to understanding the science of breeding. Every other week at the conclusion of Meredith's dressage lesson, we would recess to my kitchen. There, for the next 10 months, over iced tea and nacho chips, or cocoa and popcorn, depending on the season, she educated me based on her experiences as a veterinarian and a successful sport horse breeder.

Our discussions enhanced my personal knowledge for the breeding of my own mare. Each of our work sessions followed a progressive order on all aspects of breeding. Realizing that there were no certainties in horse breeding, we tried to explore a wide range of scenarios for every stage of the process from "perfect world" to "brink of disaster."

As the time to breed Anastasia approached, she was fit and in excellent health. My mare had always been an easy keeper. Her daily pre-pregnancy diet was divided into 3 regular feedings consisting of one-third bale of timothy hay, eight pounds of 12 percent sweet feed privately blended by my local feed mill, one ounce of Clovite supplement that was replaced by two ounces of Farnam Mare Plus as we prepared to breed, and one- quarter cup Uckele Coco-Soya oil to top dress her feed. She also spent three hours a day turned out on lush grass pasture.

Anastasia had been saddle broken the previous August as a 3-year-old, and she was in light training. This was continued four times a week. On days when Anastasia offered that special feeling under saddle, I was tempted to shelve the breeding plans and redirect our energies toward the show ring. However, determined to stick with the original plan, I knew it would be even harder to take a foaling time-out in the midst of a successful show career.

Because my goals did not require an early season foal, I planned to breed Anastasia in April. We would be using fresh-cooled semen shipped from the breeder's farm in Washington that would necessitate some schedule coordination with Vivaldi's owners as the time drew near.

An important key to recognizing the best time to breed Anastasia was a dependable in-barn teaser. At the time that I decided to breed my mare I owned a handsome, imported Grand Prix Hanoverian gelding named Wayne. (Really, that was the official name on his German papers. His sire had been named Western Star, so my best guess was that Wayne's breeder thought she had created the second coming of John Wayne.)

Anastasia's favorite teaser at Full Cry Farm was Wayne, a Hanoverian gelding trained to Grand Prix, who was proud and eager to do his duty.

Obviously, Anastasia was in agreement with that scenario, as Wayne was the only gelding in my barn to whom she overtly responded when in heat. In fact, in Wayne's presence, she became a brazen hussy. For his part, Wayne was more than proud to fulfill his teasing duties with throaty encouraging nickers and neck nuzzling over the fence, making it easy to tell when my mare was in heat.

However, as the horse business goes, one of my students purchased Wayne a month before Anastasia was to be bred. This usually happy transaction resulted in a predicament for me when the new owner prepared to move Wayne to her home stable. Despite all persuasive attempts, Anastasia was disinterested in all the other horses in my barn. It had to be Wayne as her teaser, or no one.

As a last ditch effort to retain my successful teaser, I offered Wayne's new owner a month of free board if she would allow him to stay at my farm through Anastasia's next cycle. Everyone's plans were put on hold while we waited for Anastasia to come back into heat. With so much responsibility on his broad back, we wondered if Wayne would lay claim to the resultant foal!

Chapter 6

Breeding the Mare

While some mare owners still elect to breed their horses using live cover, for the purposes of our journey, we will focus on artificial insemination as it is the predominant reproductive method utilized by sport horse breeders. AI provides stallion and mare owners with many distinct advantages over live cover.

By comparison, artificial insemination provides mare and stallion owners significant advantages over live cover:

1. The procedure offers far greater physical safety for all participants.

2. Stallion owners achieve much greater efficiency by being able to breed more mares from one collection. Capitalizing on the ability to stretch the collection to multiple mares an owner can expand her stallion's annual book without overtaxing her horse. It also makes it easier for the stallion to have both competitive and breeding careers at the same time.

3. The quality of the stallion's semen can be evaluated on collection before inseminating the mare.

4. Antibiotics are added to the extender when transporting semen to enhance the longevity of the sperm and to limit the transmission of bacterial contaminants to the mare.

5. Mare owners can avoid the inconvenience and risk of transporting their valuable mares and foals to the stallion's farm. The physical stress of the trip and the potential exposure to disease are eliminated.

6. The speed and efficiency of transported fresh-cooled semen expands the mare owner's choice of stallions to a nationwide gene pool. In addition, mare owners who are willing to accept a lower pregnancy rate by using frozen semen, have limitless access to a worldwide stallion market barring governmental importation restrictions.

Although AI is commonly used by sport horse breeders, there are still some breed registries such as The Jockey Club that do not recognize thoroughbred foals produced by this method of breeding, whether done on site or through transported semen. Be sure to familiarize yourself with the allowable practices of your chosen registry before deciding on the method with which you will breed your mare.

While the proponents of live cover argue that it is more cost efficient and generally results in a higher percentage of pregnancies than AI, the disadvantages appear to outweigh the advantages for many mare owners:

1. Live cover presents an inherent risk to the mare, stallion and handlers participating in the very physical act of breeding a pair of 1,000-plus pound horses.

2. Live cover is inconvenient for mare owners because the mare must be transported to the stallion's location for breeding. Frequently, the mare has a young foal at her side, which compounds the difficulties and risks of transportation, subjecting both of them to the hazards of a foreign farm environment.

3. Ideally with live cover, when the mare is receptive to the stallion, she should be bred once every other day for a total of three breedings. In order to achieve the best odds of catching your mare at the right time in her cycle, it is advisable to stable her at the stallion's farm during the period in which you plan to breed. This results in additional costs for board, mare care and veterinarian fees, in addition to the breeding fees.

4. Live cover makes it impossible to test and ascertain the quality of the stallion's semen. There is also a higher risk of contamination to your mare from potential pathogens in the pure ejaculate.

As with most equine ventures, the success of your breeding program directly correlates with the expertise of the personnel involved on both the stallion and mare teams. Veterinarians implementing AI should be skilled and confident in the technique. Do not allow your mare to be the training ground for an inexperienced vet.

For some people with the right mare and the right veterinarian who is dedicated to devoting the time and technique necessary to obtain a pregnancy, frozen semen can be the right choice. Some preferred stallions may only be available to your mare through frozen semen due to restrictions imposed by competition schedules or health issues. Frozen semen also provides a unique opportunity to breed to deceased stallions whose semen has been stored. Semen properly stored in liquid nitrogen may remain viable for 30 years or more.

Breeding with frozen semen may be more convenient as you can often purchase unguaranteed doses for less than guaranteed fresh-cooled semen. There is no timetable or risk of shipping delays. The shipment can be kept indefinitely in a liquid nitrogen storage tank at your veterinarian's clinic until your mare is ready to be inseminated.

However, even with the best veterinarian and a mare who appears to be a likely candidate, the overall success rate is statistically lower for frozen semen than with other means of breeding. In addition, the economic risk is far greater with the use of frozen semen. If the frozen semen must be purchased on an unguaranteed, individual dosage basis rather than a live-foal guarantee as is the case with most European and many stateside breeding contracts, repeated breedings with lack of success will have profound economic repercussions that may blow your budget sky-high with possibly no foal to show for your efforts.

As you prepare to breed your mare, keep a journal of your preparation and breeding activities. No matter how good your memory, nothing beats a well-organized log. It will provide a handy reference guide to assist you throughout the season as well as when planning future breedings.

Generally speaking, due to the advanced science and additional time involved in breeding with AI, each step taken away from live cover increases costs and lowers conception averages.

To maintain acceptable fertility of the semen, the mare should be inseminated within 24–48 hours of collection. A decreasing motility scale based on the time elapsed after collection will vary with each stallion. While the very rare individual may produce semen that remains viable up to five days after collection, be aware that no matter what the stallion owner claims, prolonged viability of the sperm is the exception rather than the norm. The fertility of some stallions may be further reduced with cooled semen and particularly with frozen semen.

If the mare does not ovulate within 48 hours of insemination, you will have to rebreed her immediately or wait until her next cycle. Plan in advance for all eventualities because immediate rebreeding will necessitate a second collection and shipment from the stallion within two days of the first breeding. The cooperation of the stallion owner is essential, but sometimes it may be difficult to accomplish with breeding farms that adhere to a strict collection schedule. Read your breeding contract carefully to know what is possible.

Sperm are vulnerable to the environmental conditions of light, temperature and chemicals. Extenders are used in the collected shipment to stabilize and protect the sperm from these adverse conditions as well as to prevent bacterial infection from being passed to the mare. However, some mares may have an adverse physical reaction to the extender that is used to prepare semen for fresh-cooled shipment. In response to certain extenders, the mare's uterus may become inflamed, creating a hostile environment for the embryo and making implantation difficult.

Mares exhibiting this reaction are not good candidates for fresh-cooled or frozen semen without changes in the extender product or a post-breeding uterine treatment. A drug called Settle (Bioniche) has been developed to be given intravenously or intra-uterine immediately prior to breeding to decrease uterine inflammatory reactions. Your veterinarian should determine if your mare is a candidate for this drug.

Semen transport containers also can affect the fertility of the shipment. Not all containers are equally effective for maintaining an adequate shipping environment. An unstable cooling environment may compromise fertility. On receipt of the container, be sure to check that it has been properly sealed and that the seal is still intact after transport. Do *not* open the container until your vet arrives to breed your mare. The shipping container should contain the following helpful information to aid your veterinarian: stallion's name (especially if the shipment is from a farm with multiple breeding stallions), time of collection, concentration of the sperm, viability of the sperm at collection and motility percentage.

Insemination timing is even more critical when breeding with frozen semen. Careful monitoring of the estrus cycle is required, potentially several times per day when ovulation is imminent. Your mare should be inseminated no earlier than 12 hours *prior* to ovulation or 8 hours immediately following ovulation. New protocols are being developed to make the timing of breeding with frozen semen more user friendly.

Mention should be made of two potentially threatening sexually transmitted diseases that may be passed from the stallion to your mare whether using fresh or frozen semen. Be sure to ascertain the stallion's status concerning the following conditions prior to signing a breeding contract.

Equine Viral Arteritis Virus is a viral disease that may be spread both as a respiratory or as a venereal disease. It is possible to transmit this disease through the use of fresh-cooled or frozen semen used in artificial insemination. EVA can be responsible for abortion as well as respiratory symptoms and fever in pregnant mares. Infected mares also may be contagious to other mares in the herd or barn, spreading the virus in the form of a respiratory disease.

Should you choose to breed to an EVA-positive stallion, your mare will need to receive a protective vaccine at least three weeks prior to breeding. Recently vaccinated mares must be separated from other horses on the farm for a three-week period. Discuss with your vet whether your property has adequate space to accommodate required quarantine distances. Once the quarantine period has elapsed, your mare should be blood-tested to be certain she is adequately protected before being bred to an EVA-positive stallion or reintroduced to the mare band.

Contagious equine metritis is a bacterial infection of the genital tract. While CEM has been eradicated from North America, there is still the potential to contaminate a mare with frozen semen illegally imported from outside North America. CEM is still carried by some stallions in many European countries. Frozen semen shipments from outside North America must contain a health certificate from a licensed veterinarian at the origin of the shipment attesting to the health status of the shipment.

As you prepare to breed, if you are uncertain as to the timetable of your mare's cycle, it is a good idea to have your veterinarian conduct an exam to assess her follicular status. An experienced vet will examine the mare's reproductive tract through rectal palpation or ultrasonography. Since many mares do not appreciate this invasive procedure, sedation and/or a twitch are sometimes required to protect the handlers from injury and the equipment from damage. The exam findings will determine the size of the existing follicles to approximate the number of days until your mare ovulates. (If you have your mare checked early in the year, there may be only immature follicles present especially if she is in the transitional stage.) Your veterinarian also will check for uterine tone and the state of the mare's cervix that should be softening as she prepares to ovulate. Armed with this information, you will know when to order semen from the stallion owner.

Once you have established a baseline for the size of the existing follicle, you can estimate when your mare should ovulate. The average follicle grows at an average daily rate of .3 centimeters, but many mares ignore the law of averages and create their own growth patterns. The size of the dominant follicle at ovulation ranges from 3–7 centimeters, but the average ovulating follicle is 4–4.5 centimeters. Both ovaries may produce a dominant follicle, presenting the possibility of twins. Some mares are predisposed to twinning, so be sure your vet checks both ovaries during all preliminary exams.

Based on follicular development, when you have determined that your mare is a week away from breeding, give the owner of your contracted stallion a heads-up call to let her know your mare's status. Good communication is a must and will be greatly appreciated by the stallion owner who may be besieged by phone calls from frantic mare owners at the peak of the breeding season. When your mare is 48 hours from ovulating, you will need to make a second call to finalize the actual shipment date.

Fresh-cooled semen is generally shipped overnight the day of collection, with delivery made to your farm the following day. Breeding the mare just prior to ovulation with fresh-cooled semen provides optimal pregnancy rates. Varying time zones can effect stallion collection and shipping schedules. Without the use of hormonal chemicals to regulate your mare's cycle, your planned breeding timing may be incompatible with the stallion or Fed Ex's schedule.

Frozen semen can be shipped well in advance of the breeding date to the veterinary specialist who will inseminate your mare. The product is shipped in a special container that differs from a fresh-cooled semen container in that it contains liquid nitrogen to keep the frozen semen super cool. The breeding specialist will handle the transfer of the product and the return of the container. Unless you plan to breed your mare immediately on receipt of the container, you will need access to a special long-term storage tank containing liquid nitrogen to maintain the extremely cold temperature necessary to keep the semen viable.

Frozen semen arrives contained in small tubes called straws that may come in various sizes. The number of straws required per insemination varies by stallion. This information will be provided with the shipment. The process of thawing the semen and inseminating the mare involves precise steps in temperature control to ready the semen from a frozen state prior to insemination. Specific thawing instructions should be included with each shipment as the thawing technique will vary by stallion and product.

If you are using fresh-cooled semen, the moment of breeding your mare and the arrival of the semen-shipping container must be closely coordinated. On receipt, the container should be inspected for any external damage received in transit. Mare owners should not open the container themselves because this action will initiate the semen warming cycle. It is a good idea to have your vet examine microscopically a sample of the semen prior to insemination to check for quality, including motility and shape. If the motility does not correspond with the evaluation report supplied in the shipment by the breeder, it may reflect a problem in the handling process. Be sure to immediately discuss any discrepancies with the stallion owner.

As you prepare to breed, your vet may first sedate your mare. He will then rectally palpate her to assure the cervix is relaxed and the follicle is the appropriate size to ovulate within the next 48 hours. Once she has been inseminated, if she does not ovulate within 24 hours, the mare will need to be rebred immediately if a pregnancy is to be achieved from this cycle.

The mare's tail should be wrapped and held out of the way or tied to a rope around her neck. Cleansing the mare's external genitalia is extremely important for preventing bacterial infections that may affect her ability to maintain a pregnancy. The area should be repeatedly scrubbed with soap and rinsed until it would pass a white glove test.

There are special syringes that do not contain black rubber plungers that should be used for AI. Be aware that the black rubber plungers found in typical syringe are spermicidal. They should be avoided as this type of plunger will kill sperm on contact. Your vet will fill the special AI syringe with semen from the container. You or her assistant will then hold the syringe while she dons a sterile sleeve that covers from her hand to shoulder. Sterile, nonspermicidal lubricant will be applied to the sleeve.

A sterile AI pipette will be held protected in the veterinarian's hand and passed manually through the cervix into the mare's uterus. The syringe containing the semen is then attached to the pipette. The semen is inserted into the mare's uterus by slowly pushing the plunger. Following the insertion of the semen, the pipette is carefully withdrawn. For those choosing chemical assistance with ovulation, your mare may now receive an hCG or deslorelin injection to chemically stimulate the mare to ovulate within 12–48 hours.

The shipment from the stallion owner may contain a second packet of semen. Many mare owners feel that the mare is the best storage container and elect to inseminate her with both dosages rather than leaving the second packet in the resealed container for breeding the following day as repeated inseminations can increase the risk of infection.

Some mares have difficulty with uterine clearance of expended semen, causing it to remain pooled in the body of the uterus rather then being expelled out the cervix. Other mares may experience an inflammatory reaction to the semen or the extender. Both these types of mares may require a post-breeding uterine flush and/or injections of oxytocin to assist in cleansing the uterus. This procedure should be done no earlier than four to eight hours post-breeding. After this point, there is no risk of flushing out the embryo as the sperm is protected within the oviduct and the resultant embryo will not descend into the uterus for five days.

Mares with less-than-optimum vulvar conformation will have a Caslick procedure done at this time. The Caslick procedure does not interfere with rebreeding if it becomes necessary.

Your mare has now been bred. Be certain to schedule a recheck with your veterinarian for the following day to be certain your mare ovulates within 24 hours of insemination. When you have confirmed that she has ovulated within the acceptable time frame, all that is left to do for the next 12 – 16 days is to cross your fingers and think positive thoughts until your vet conducts an ultrasound that confirms whether all your planning and efforts have paid off.

Personal Journey

My plan was to breed for a mid–2004 spring foal. However, since Anastasia was a young, maiden mare, we knew we would be starting from scratch without a helpful comparative breeding baseline of her normal follicular activity and ovulation schedule. As Meredith was quick to remind me, a maiden mare hasn't read the breeding "how-to" book. That being the case, Anastasia and I would have to write our own personal version as we went along.

The stage was set in March for Dr. Strosnider to assist me in putting my plan in motion. On March 14, we did a trial run, checking follicular activity without breeding to establish a baseline for the "real thing" in May. Initially, Dr. Strosnider did not think we would need to use chemicals to cycle Anastasia as she exhibited very clear, regular heat cycles accentuated by an overt response to my teaser gelding, Wayne. In March and April, I carefully monitored her receptiveness, noting her interest was strongest March 12–18 and April 5–11.

The following month on May 5, when Anastasia expressed increased interest in Wayne, I called Dr. Strosnider to conduct a breeding exam. His ultrasound revealed a 4 centimeter follicle on her right ovary. Looking at the distinct spot on the ultrasound, I realized that dress rehearsals were officially over. It was showtime, and I needed to contact Three Crowns Farm.

I placed the phone call to order the semen that morning. Just to be safe, I requested a second shipment to be delivered two days later in the chance that Anastasia did not ovulate on the first insemination, necessitating immediate rebreeding. The container was to be shipped FedEx Priority Overnight with a guaranteed 8 a.m.

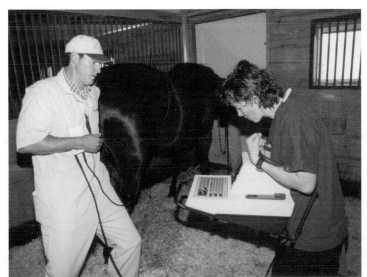

Dr. Strosnider and assistant, Jenny, check the ultrasound for follicle size and location on a breeding trial run to establish a baseline for ovulation.

The Equitainer sent by Three Crowns Farm contained two doses of Vivaldi's semen. The container remained sealed until Dr. Strosnider arrived to breed Anastasia.

delivery the following day. Hanging up the phone, I was struck by the magnitude of events I had just put into motion with a simple phone call.

The following morning Dr. Strosnider arrived at 8:30 a.m. to inseminate Anastasia, but there was no sign of FedEx. A call to the shipper's local office added another layer of stress. It appeared that my shipment had been delayed overnight in Memphis due to inclement weather. However, the phone operator assured me it was now in transit with delivery promised by 11a.m. My vet had to leave for another farm call, but promised to return when I notified him that the container had arrived. There was nothing for me to do but turn out my mare in her paddock and pace the fenceline while I waited. Anastasia grazed contentedly in the sunshine. At least one of us was totally unconcerned by the delay in plans.

Dr. Strosnider removes one of the semen packets from the Equitainer to prepare it for insemination.

At noon, both the Equitainer and my vet finally arrived together at my farm. The container held two doses that each contained, according to the packing tag, 15–20 c.c. of raw semen at 301 million sperm per milliliter of semen, exhibiting 75 percent motility at collection at 12:30 p.m. Pacific time the previous day. Dr. Strosnider inseminated Anastasia with both doses at 12:30 p.m. on a 4.5 centimeter soft follicle. On completion, he administered hCG to induce ovulation within the next 12–48 hours.

When Dr. Strosnider returned the next morning to palpate Anastasia, we were disappointed to discover that she had not ovulated. The follicle had grown to 5 centimeters and was quite soft. I was glad I'd had the foresight to order a second shipment due to arrive by 8 a.m. the next morning.

This time the weather cooperated and FedEx arrived on time. Dr. Strosnider palpated Anastasia at 8:30 a.m. to ascertain she had not ovulated overnight. On this check, the follicle was now 5-plus centimeters and extremely soft. He rebred her, confident that this time we would be successful.

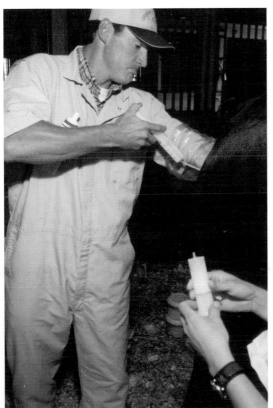

The following afternoon at 4:00 p.m. Dr. Strosnider returned to check her status. To our delight, she had ovulated. Right on schedule…this time! Now the wait began to see if our efforts had been successful.

On May 27, 17 days post-ovulation, Dr. Strosnider returned to ultrasound Anastasia to see if she was pregnant. However, search as he might, the scan did not show any evidence of an embryo. He rechecked her at 21 days just to be certain that we had not missed it, but to no avail. Back to the drawing board.

Dr. Strosnider carefully inseminates Anastasia with the first of two dosage syringes.

In Anastasia's case, it required a trial run through a breeding cycle to determine she ovulated off a large 5-plus centimeter follicle. Because she teased very responsively early in her cycle, it was easy to be fooled by her overt receptiveness to Wayne. Obviously, relying on Nature's indications was not going to work for us.

Although we did not use hormones to regulate her cycle on the first attempt, after the failed effort, I decided to change strategy. I determined that despite the added expense for the products, the predictability of the hormones far offset my rising veterinary and stallion collection/shipping expenses created by additional breedings. In the conflict of nature vs. science, I decided to side with science.

On June 2, I started Anastasia on a daily regimen of 11 cc of Regumate squirted on her morning sweet feed. This was continued until June 11 when I administered 2 cc of prostaglandin (Lytalyse). At this time, the Regumate was discontinued.

On June 16, Anastasia was ultrasounded to reveal good uterine tone and a 2.5 centimeter follicle on her right ovary. The next ultrasound on June 18 showed a 3 centimeter follicle that was softening. Dr. Strosnider suggested I order the semen.

On June 20, Anastasia was bred off a 5.1 centimeter follicle. On completion of the insemination, Dr. Strosnider inserted an Ovuplant into the skin of the external lip of her vulva. This chemical implant of deslorelin (GnRH) is known to induce ovulation within 48 hours of insertion with an extremely high predictability. The dissolving implant required removal shortly after ovulation or within 48 hours of insertion.

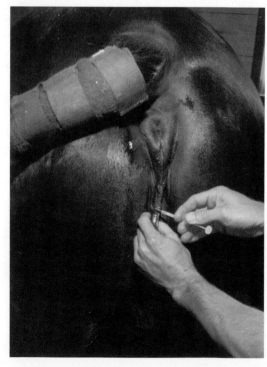

An Ovuplant is inserted by Dr. Strosnider immediately post-breeding to help induce ovulation within 48 hours.

On June 21, Dr. Strosnider ultrasounded to find she had ovulated. The vet check coincided with the FedEx delivery of a second fresh shipment of semen. Just to be certain that all of our bases were covered, we inseminated her again in case she had just ovulated. Before leaving, my vet removed the Ovuplant.

Eighteen days later, on July 9, amidst much finger crossing and wishing on stars, Dr. Strosnider returned to ultrasound for the pregnancy check. With very little searching, the screen unmistakably revealed an embryonic vesicle in the right horn. Hooray! We celebrated a mission accomplished but tempered our elation with caution as there was still a long, uncertain road ahead.

As the first trimester is such an unpredictable period, a series of ultrasound checks are advised to be certain the mare retains the pregnancy.
On July 22, Dr. Strosnider conducted the second of three early pregnancy checks. I think the biggest thrill of the pregnancy came on day 32 when for the first time I actually saw a fetal heartbeat on the ultrasound monitor. All my hopes and dreams steadily beating in that little sport horse heart. It was quite overpowering. Only my vet giving my shoulder a congratulatory squeeze brought my feet back down to the ground.

The final ultrasound was done on August 19, 61 days into the pregnancy. This check revealed the appearance of a normally developing fetus and placenta. While nothing in a pregnancy is a certainty until the foal is born, we felt we had surpassed a big hurdle and were well on our way to an approximate due date of May 26, 2004.

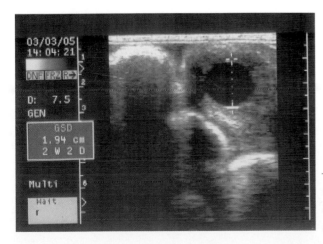

After years of planning, nothing could compare with my thrill of seeing the 18-day old embryo on the ultrasound pregnancy check.

Chapter 7

Managing the Pregnant Mare
The First 300 Days

Two weeks have passed since your mare was bred—a very long two weeks of waiting and wondering. Her daily behavior throughout this period has become the primary focus of your life. You watch carefully for the appearance of that mellow glaze of pregnancy in contrast to any physical indication that she may be coming back into heat. Sometimes it seems that she is watching you with equal intensity as she haughtily guards her grand secret—a special secret that she does not have to divulge until the vet comes for her first pregnancy check between days 14–18.

A series of pregnancy checks are recommended at two-week intervals in the first few months post-breeding to ascertain pregnancy and then to follow its development. Barring unforeseen circumstances, mares who retain their pregnancy beyond 60 days tend to carry the fetus to full term. Beyond your personal interest, check the breeding contract to be sure you fulfill the stallion owner's contractual requirements for confirming the various stages of your mare's pregnancy.

While rectal ultrasonography provides the earliest detection of pregnancy, rectal palpation is the most common and cost-efficient method of checking your mare. Pregnancy determination utilizing rectal palpation is extremely difficult in the first 18 days due to the extremely small size of the embryonic vesicle. However, in the earliest days, rectal palpation can still detect the pregnancy indicators of increased uterine tone as well as the closing and tightening of the cervix. By Day 25, it is possible to palpate a spherical bulge, approximately the size of a golf ball or a hen's egg, on one of the uterine horns.

To guarantee the best chance of accuracy, it is highly recommended that the first pregnancy check be conducted between days 14–18 utilizing transrectal ultrasound. Your aim is to achieve two critical points of discovery on this important check. First, can a viable pregnancy be identified? You are searching for a tiny, black sphere called an embryonic vesicle that is highly mobile for the first 17 days after creation.

The embryonic vesicle will migrate throughout the entire uterus before finally implanting in one of the uterine horns. Scanning with the ultrasound for a tiny 12–22 millimeter sphere can be harder than searching for a needle in a haystack. Despite the best equipment, you and your vet can just plain miss it! The embryonic vesicle also can be confused with a uterine cyst, especially if your mare was not ultrasounded prior to breeding to identify the location of any permanent cysts.

The second consideration on the first pregnancy check is to rule out the presence of twins. In your excitement to discover the embryonic vesicle, your veterinarian should not stop searching until the entire uterus has been carefully scanned to determine that there is no second vesicle present. Some mares are genetically predisposed to twinning. If you know your mare falls into this category or this is her first foal, be on high alert during her initial pregnancy check.

In the case of twins, if the embryonic vesicles are immediately adjacent in the same uterine horn, many mares will correct the condition themselves after day 17. However, if the vesicles are located in opposite horns of the uterus, the mare's body will not recognize a problem with the condition and the pregnancy will continue as twins. Your veterinarian will advise you when and if it is advisable to intervene and pinch off one of the vesicles. If the vesicles are immediately adjacent, pinching off must be accomplished prior to fixation in the wall of the uterine horn while they are still in a mobile condition prior to day 17. Pinching off after day 17 up to day 30 is more difficult, depending on the location of the fixation of the vesicles.

If two normally shaped embryos are still visible on the second ultrasound pregnancy check at between day 28–30, your vet still may attempt to pinch off the smaller embryo if accessible, or he may advise you to terminate the pregnancy and start over. If you are unsuccessful in pinching off the embryo or you fail to identify twins early in the pregnancy, the majority of mares will resolve the condition themselves because a horse's uterus is not designed to carry two large fetuses to term. In many cases, both fetuses may die and be aborted or one may die and mummify, leaving the strongest to survive.

If a pregnancy is not detected on the first check, do not be totally discouraged. Schedule your veterinarian to return to ultrasound again within a week in case the vesicle was missed the first time around. If a pregnancy is still not detected on the recheck, you may elect to chemically recycle your mare to prepare for rebreeding or simply allow her to come back into heat, which should occur naturally 21 days after her last ovulation.

If the initial check confirms a pregnancy, your veterinarian should re-ultrasound in two weeks to be sure the mare has retained the embryo. This is a very fragile period until the embryonic vesicle implants in the uterine horn. If the mare has maintained a viable pregnancy, by this second check you should be able to see the fetal heartbeat, which is quite a thrill.

A third pregnancy check is advised in another two weeks. At this point, your pregnant mare will have formed structures in her uterus called endometrial cups that secrete a hormone known as equine chorionic gonadotropin (eCG). This hormone is necessary for embryo maintenance. Less than 10 percent of pregnancies are lost once these cups have formed. However, if pregnancy loss does occur after the formation of the endometrial cups, it will be too late to rebreed in the same season. The mare will not return to normal estrus until the cups degenerate in approximately three months.

Many veterinarians recommend, and stallion contracts require, a final pregnancy verification at two months. While ultrasound is an effective tool in diagnosing early pregnancy and its progress, after two months rectal palpation is most commonly used. Beyond day 60, it becomes difficult to visualize the fetus on the ultrasound screen due to its increasing size and the progressive enlargement of the uterus that moves it beyond the veterinarian's reach.

Most people are curious about the gender of their fetus. Your vet can solve the mystery after day 105 by using a transrectal ultrasound that has a special 5-megahertz transducer. Sexing the foal is a special skill, requiring your vet to have training beyond standard ultrasound reading.

An extra pregnancy check may be done at day 150 to confirm that the mare has maintained her pregnancy. If the check is positive, you mare should receive the first of three rhinopneumonitis EHV-1 vaccinations. Be sure to mark your calendar for the necessary follow-up boosters of this important abortion preventing vaccine to be given additionally in the seventh and ninth months.

In a normal pregnancy, between day 50–70, the fetal placenta assists the mare by beginning self-production of progesterone. By day 150, the fetal placenta assumes the complete responsibility for producing the progesterone necessary to maintain the pregnancy to term.

There is some concern regarding mares who initially conceive only to lose the embryo at a very early stage due to the mare's inability to produce sufficient progesterone to maintain her pregnancy. This condition is known to occur in young mares (ages 5 and younger) who are sexually immature. It also may affect senior mares (age 15 and older) who may require progesterone supplementation as they age to help maintain their pregnancies as well as to prevent late term abortions.

If your veterinarian feels your mare falls into the low-progesterone-producing risk category, you may want to run a progesterone assay to compare her levels against normal. If she tests below the normal range, you may elect to start her on a 120-day course of Regumate until the fetal placenta takes over the job of producing the progesterone for the balance of the pregnancy. An even longer course of Regumate may be recommended for the senior mare, maintaining her on the product virtually up to parturition.

As your mare progresses through the months of her pregnancy, it is hard to visualize the size of the growing fetus within her. Particularly in the early months, except for a softening of her eye and a general aura of tranquility, her outward appearance will be virtually unchanged. However, as you groom her coat that shines with a new luster from the pregnancy hormones or watch her graze peacefully in the pasture, the following growth list may help you understand the developing size of what your mare is carrying:

Comparable Fetus Sizes

Day 60–hamster

Day 80–chipmunk

Day 100–6-week-old kitten

Day 150–rabbit

Day 240–lamb

Day 270–German shepherd

Some mares become "professional broodmares," spending idyllic years wandering lush pastures, their sole job to create and nurture a succession of foals. These mares spend the peaceful months of pregnancy as munching lawn ornaments until four to six weeks prior to their foaling dates. At this point, they should be brought in from full-time pasture to be immunized with their annual boosters. While they may remain on some form of pasture, late-term broodmares should be accessible for regular observation as their due dates approach.

On the other hand, some mares are "working girls," destined for the competition arena. These mares may be young maidens who are having a foal before serious training begins or seasoned campaigners who are taking a break from their regular performance jobs before age becomes a negating factor in the pregnancy process. In both these cases, the intent is to return the mare to the show ring after the birth and weaning of her foal.

The old horseman's adage "motion is lotion" holds true for pregnant mares as well as for aging equine athletes. Some form of exercise is beneficial for your pregnant mare even if it is only free access to pasture. While some owners share casual trail rides with their pregnant mares, the owners of "working girls" may elect to keep them in training until the sixth month, or as long as the mare can comfortably tolerate the required level of exercise.

However, as pregnancy progresses, it will be necessary to downscale her exercise program to suit the changing comfort level dictated by her condition until she reaches the point of retiring barefoot to the pasture to wait out her term. Mares generally will tell you when they have reached the work reduction point. All you have to do is pay attention and read their body language. However, whatever their state of pregnancy or level of work, all mares will enjoy a therapeutic massage to stimulate blood flow and relax taxed muscles.

If you elect to continue light riding into your mare's final trimester, be very conscious of the quality of footing as her natural balance will be changing along with her condition. It is important to avoid any exercise stress that may result in a fall. Also, avoid introducing any new levels of activity and do not push her work to the point of exhaustion.

Caring for your pregnant mare requires regular observation of her changing physical status and resultant physical level. However, despite our best conscientious efforts, some pregnancies are spontaneously terminated in the very early stages. Factors that can influence early embryonic death include hormonal deficiencies in the mare, a hostile uterine environment, embryonic genetic defects or external environmental triggers including stress, poor nutrition and the season of the year. If your mare experiences EED, you and your veterinarian need to quickly address cycling her again while there is still time if you plan to rebreed in the same season.

While most pregnancies beyond day 60 progress smoothly through parturition, you are strongly advised to educate yourself to detect the most common pregnancy-loss triggers should that eventuality occur. These triggers may initially present as behavioral changes or physical abnormalities. Pregnancy loss triggers can be categorized as embryonic factors, maternal factors or external factors:

Embryonic factors. Embryos are genetically preprogrammed by the mare and the stallion at conception to follow a normal developmental course. If there are chromosome abnormalities in the foal's genetic make-up, they may disrupt some of the key triggers for cell division. In this irreparable scenario, the foal may be born with deformities or be aborted during the term of the pregnancy.

During your mare's second pregnancy check, ultrasonography makes it possible to identify genetic abnormalities by recognizing normal versus abnormal shape of the embryonic vesicle. If there is a serious problem, you will probably discover that your mare has reabsorbed the abnormal vesicle by the third pregnancy check.

It is important for the embryo to implant in the right location in the uterus. If the embryo mistakenly implants in the uterine body rather than in the uterine horn, the condition must be recognized and terminated by your veterinarian by day 35. The mare's body will not notice or rectify improper implantation. If left uncorrected, the pregnancy will continue to develop in the uterine body only to end in abortion later in gestation. The limited growth space of the uterine body prevents a full term pregnancy.

Maternal factors. The mare's physiology bears the bulk of the responsibility for maintaining the pregnancy. In addition to twinning and low progesterone levels, you should be aware of additional maternal pregnancy-loss triggers.

The status of the uterine environment should be of primary concern throughout the pregnancy. The uterus can be contaminated by negative components such as bacteria or dirt that may be introduced through a cervical defect, poor vulvar conformation or human intervention during the insemination process. Infectious placentitis occurs when the mare is exposed to bacteria, viruses or some fungal organisms. In this condition, the placenta becomes infected and malfunctions, directly contaminating the fetus. The result is abortion, stillbirth, premature delivery or growth retardation. The most common outward sign of this condition is premature lactation. If your mare begins to stream milk well before her due date, immediately contact your veterinarian. With prompt attention, specific antibiotics and hormones may be able to save the pregnancy.

Try to protect your mare from severe abdominal injuries such as a kick or a fall, which can disrupt her pregnancy. A fall, the simple action of rolling or even movement by the foal in mid to late term may result in a serious condition known as uterine torsion. If the uterus becomes twisted, blood flow will be restricted to the organ. The condition will present as colic. Surgery may be required to correct the twist.

The health of the mare will have a direct affect on the well-being of the embryo. Any metabolic diseases such as hypothyroidism or diabetes adversely affect the mare's ability to become pregnant or to maintain a foal to term. If you recognize a questionable condition in your mare, immediately consult your veterinarian regarding a physical exam and possible lab work-up to identify and treat the problem.

External factors. External environmental factors can provoke powerful pregnancy-loss triggers. The primary causes can be found in the physiological and emotional stresses that confront your mare in her daily life. Stress is a particularly powerful pregnancy-loss trigger. A change in routine such as leaving the security of her home farm to be bred or to compete in a horse show or to participate in a clinic during her pregnancy can threaten the health of the unborn foal. Trailering can be stressful to any horse, but particularly on a newly pregnant mare. It is often advised to avoid trailering if at all possible until the pregnancy is well established after the first trimester.

Any routine or environmental change that exposes the mare to outside contaminants and viruses not found in her home stable can threaten the pregnancy. Not only can the mare come into contact with threatening foreign contaminants by visiting the breeding farm or showgrounds, but she is also at risk from exposure to viruses introduced by outside horses who may visit her home stable.

If your mare requires any medical treatment, make sure the treating veterinarian is aware that she is pregnant as well as her breeding date so he will know how far she is into the pregnancy. Be sure to consult with your veterinarian regarding the safety of any drugs or supplements to be used during the pregnancy. For example, xylazine (Rompun) and flunixin meglumine (Banamine) should be avoided in late term as either may induce labor.

Another jeopardizing environmental contaminant comes from fescue pasture grass and hay. The endophyte fungus acremonium may contaminate some fescue. If this fungus is ingested by a pregnant mare 60–90 days prior to foaling, fescue toxicosis may cause prolonged gestation with subsequent difficulty delivering oversized, weak or stillborn foals. It also may be responsible for poor colostrum levels in the mare's milk. Not all fescue is contaminated. If you must feed fescue, it is advised to have it tested annually for the presence of the contaminant before exposing your mare. If your feed source is infected, alternate means of feeding must be used until the mare delivers. In addition, to prevent low milk production, the mare should remain off infected fescue until after weaning.

As the mare's caretaker, you bear the ultimate responsibility for the outcome of her pregnancy. It is important that you pay careful attention to details by considering all the underlying factors can make or break the success of your venture. While it may be impossible to control all of the negative factors that may affect your mare during her pregnancy, many can be minimized or totally avoided through diligent observation and positive action. Your mare and unborn foal are counting on you!

Personal Journey

Anastasia was started in training at 3 ½ years old, six months prior to breeding. From her first long-line lesson, she was a willing training partner, eager to please and quick to respond. I hoped that her eager acceptance of basic training was a harbinger of the traits she would pass on to her offspring. Once working quietly under saddle, I proceeded to introduce basic dressage training, continuing through her sixth month of pregnancy with a focus on suppleness, obedience and simple transitions.

At five months pregnant, Anastasia was glowing and fit in the October sun.

However, over the Christmas holiday, it became evident that Anastasia was no longer enamored with carrying me in addition to her growing foal. She was not shy about informing me of the need to change our exercise routine by pinning her ears and growing progressively crankier to my leg and weight pressure. Acquiescing to her needs, I discontinued riding on January 1, but continued light lungeing in addition to daily turnout to help keep her fit and toned.

To ease her discomfort during the pregnancy, I enlisted the services of the massage therapist who worked on my competition horses. From the first session, Anastasia loved the therapeutic addition to her routine. She became so proficient at receiving massages that she actively directed the therapist's actions by insistently repositioning her body whenever she felt the therapist was not working in the right location. Needless to say, a deep massage was truly a treat in the final months as she slowed down, becoming more and more encumbered by her foal.

When Anastasia was a developing filly, I had shown her in-hand at breed shows to expose her to unfamiliar competition surroundings where she would one day go to work as a riding horse. However, once her pregnancy was confirmed, I elected to keep her at home to avoid contact with potentially threatening outside contaminants.

Six months prior to breeding, Anastasia developed inflammation in her left eye that initially presented as tearing with a growing haze that gradually developed over her cornea. When normal anti-inflammatory treatments prescribed by my farm vet were unsuccessful in resolving the condition, I consulted an ophthalmologic specialist. She determined that she had contracted a herpes virus in her eye. We treated it aggressively with steroid drops. Fortunately, the condition resolved itself a month prior to breeding with no permanent damage to the eye. We were able to discontinue the steroids with no further flare-ups. I carefully monitored the eye throughout her pregnancy, but there was no sign of reoccurrence.

When Anastasia was confirmed pregnant, Meredith suggested that I put her on a 120-day course of Regumate. Since my mare was a young maiden, we wanted to insure she had adequate progesterone levels to sustain the growing embryo until it could naturally produce the hormone. I never questioned the added expense of Meredith's suggestions if it could improve my chances of getting a healthy, full-term foal.

The balance of Anastasia's pregnancy was uneventful as she contentedly wandered her pasture. Her human contact centered on being spoiled with treats, grooming and compliments. She thoroughly enjoyed the extra attention and begged for more. However, as the time passed and her size swelled with the nearing due date, I sensed she began to impatiently check off the days on a stall calendar to mark the time when she could return to the physical freedom of bucking playfully around her field and teasing the geldings over the fence.

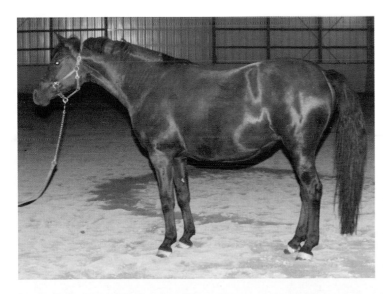

In March, Anastasia entered her tenth month rounder and more subdued, but definitely still glowing from the healthy hormones of pregnancy.

Chapter 8

Pregnant Mare Time
The Final 40 Days

Hopefully, you and your mare have made it successfully through the mellow middle months of pregnancy to arrive at the final 40 days. At this point, she is extremely pregnant, shuffling with a sometimes-awkward sway and ever-increasing lethargy. She almost seems to regard you over the pasture fence with a long, fixed stare that explicitly says, "What were you thinking? How could you do this to me?" That look reminds you that it is time to make your final preparations for the big day.

The most predictable aspect of determining your mare's foaling time is the unpredictable nature of your mission. Despite our best efforts to time things out, mares seem determined to control this final phase of their pregnancy. Do not trust that due date on your breeding calendar because mares are extremely skillful at being secretive. It is ironic that the more you attempt to manage your mare's delivery time, the more she will find ways to frustrate you by delaying the inevitable.

Do not expect to be lucky enough to fall into the perfect world scenario of a healthy foal born at 9 a.m. on a sunny morning while you are patiently waiting outside her stall. Unfortunately, Mother Nature governs that the majority of mares foal in the depths of night between 11 p.m. and 4 a.m. Your life for the next 40 days will be governed by "Pregnant Mare Time," with your mare controlling the clock.

Step up your vigilance beginning around day 300 in the event that she delivers early. Move your observations into high gear during the final three weeks in order to recognize any deviation from her normal routine. Keep a daily log, recording any physical or behavioral changes as they occur.

Normal gestation is considered between 320–365 days with 340 days the average. Be aware that a foal who arrives before day 320 is considered premature and may require extensive veterinary assistance to survive and thrive. On the other hand, do not be surprised if your mare slides right past her anticipated due date, especially if she is a maiden with no previous foaling history. Foals due in the winter or early spring may go 10 days beyond the expected norm due to seasonal factors. Colts may have a delivery date two to three days later than fillies. As you can see, there are no hard-and-fast rules on which you can depend. However, if your mare experiences prolonged gestation beyond day 365, consult with your veterinarian as to whether there is cause for concern requiring her involvement.

Although you may begin to feel that your life and that of your family is at the mercy of "Pregnant Mare Time," there are still many factors that you can control as you enter the final 40 days.

Booster shots and worming. Be sure to update your mare on her annual vaccinations four to six weeks prior to her anticipated due date. The basic booster injection series for pregnant mare should include: Eastern and Western equine encephalomyelitis, tetanus, West Nile and influenza. If your pregnant mare is apt to become exposed to other diseases from visiting outside facilities or contacting newly arrived horses, discuss the best course of protective action with your vet. The newborn foal will receive its initial disease immunity directly through its dam's colostrum. The mare should receive a final worming no closer than 30 days prior to her foaling date.

Caslick removed by day 300. If you mare has a Caslick, resist the temptation to open it earlier than day 300 because it is still serving its function of protecting the uterine environment from outside contaminants. However, if you delay beyond day 300 and your foal arrives early, the delivery will forcibly tear your mare's vulva, causing much damage and discomfort. Your veterinarian may wish to locally anesthetize your mare to perform the simple surgical procedure that opens the suture line in the vulva.

Body condition. As your mare's foaling date draws near, be sure she maintains adequate body weight. A mare's appetite tends to wane in the final days of pregnancy due to the pressure of the growing foal on her internal organs. As a result, dietary fat supplementation such as corn oil or rice bran may be required to provide adequate calories to sustain her condition. You also may want to consider adding a bran mash to her menu to stimulate her appetite or to help if she becomes constipated.

You can expect your mare to drop weight after foaling due to the demands of nursing. The caloric needs of the new mother skyrocket during the first three months of milk production. Her personal dietary needs should rebalance after this initial period as the foal begins to seek the majority of its calories from outside food sources.

Stall and property preparation. If you have decided to move your mare to a professional foaling-out facility, your last responsibility is to hitch up the trailer and drop her off at the site a month prior to her due date. On the plus side of this decision, you will be guaranteed regular work and sleep patterns until you receive a phone call from the foaling farm manager inviting you to visit your newly arrived foal and his or her proud mother.

However, if you are among the majority of mare owners opting for home delivery, it is time to address your final facility preparations. There is a great debate over field versus stall foaling. Outdoor foaling can be a positive experience if the environment is clean, dry and warm, with easy human access for intervention, if necessary, in case of emergency. An open outdoor area allows the mare more unrestricted space as she goes into labor. In addition, grassy fields have less bacterial and fungal contaminants to infect the newborn than do enclosed stalls.

However, in pasture foalings where other horses are present, there is always the chance of physical danger to the foal from another mare. Also, there is the risk that another mare may steal the newborn. If this occurs right after birth, it may result in a lack of bonding between the foal and its mother. As a consequence, the foal may not receive the necessary and very important immunity-boosting colostrum in the first hours after birth. Cold, wet or insect-infested outdoor conditions may also jeopardize the newborn's start to life.

Inside foaling guarantees you much greater control over your mare's environment and immediate access in case of emergency. Be sure your foaling stall contains adequate open space of at least 10 feet by 20 feet. Beware of dangerous projections at the foal's level, including bucket hooks, screw eyes, construction bolts or nails that could wound or blind a newborn. Water buckets and feed tubs should be removable and hung off the floor. Close any existing gaps between boards, under stall doors or between divider bars that could entrap a tiny hoof. You may want to consider closing off access to adjoining stalls with foal-safe mesh or boards. Some mares may benefit from full or partial privacy walls between adjoining stalls to eliminate the stress caused by curious neighbors.

If you regularly bed stalls with wood shavings, switch to clean straw by day 320 so you are prepared if the foal arrives early. Your goal is a dust-free environment to protect the newborn's vulnerable respiratory system. Clean straw is the bedding of choice because it does not harbor bacteria or dust particles that can infect a newborn's lungs or umbilical site or potentially harm the postpartum mare who is susceptible to infection. Wait 10 days to two weeks after foaling before returning to bedding with shavings

The ideal stall base provides good traction and drainage. It should be covered with straw. Although rubber mats simplify stall cleaning, they present a potential traction danger to the newborn struggling to stand because the surface is extremely slippery when wet. Be smart when bedding with straw. What seems like luxurious bedding to your eyes may cause stressful struggles for your newborn if it is too deep. Bank the stall walls with straw, and only bed the center deep enough for a comfortable cushion, but not so deep that your new foal disappears. Be diligent about keeping the stall clean. Pick it regularly throughout the day to keep it free of manure and urine.

Many mares who reside outside are herdbound and easily stressed by separation anxiety when they are brought into the stable as their foaling dates near. If this is the case with your mare, delay herd separation until day 320. You also may want to consider putting a pasture buddy from her herd in the adjoining stall if your mare is lonely or does not adjust to indoor confinement. The companion will provide familiarity that will help to alleviate her anxiety.

Whatever your foaling location of choice, the mare should occupy it for two weeks prior to her due date. Disinfect the foaling stall with bleach before the mare takes up residence. If she is turned out in a paddock during the day, be sure she returns to the same stall in the evening. The mare will need to acclimate to the foaling area and create antibodies to the specific environmental organisms. These antibodies will be passed on through her colostrum as protection for her newborn foal.

Horses are most relaxed in a darkened nighttime environment. If your mare goes into labor at night, you do not want to startle her by throwing on the barn lights. However, as you will need the assistance of some light to observe her, let her gradually acclimate to all-night soft light by leaving a low-watt stall light on every night for two weeks prior to the delivery date. The constant light will help to eliminate unnecessary surprises for her and for you when the big moment occurs. If you do not want to use all-night stable lighting for observation, another option is a night-vision remote camera that will allow you to follow her behavior without intrusive lighting.

Careful observation, immediate access to your veterinarian's phone number and the ability to survive long, sleepless nights while maintaining your good humor will be your best tools through the final few weeks. If you pay attention, you will recognize physical signs presented by your mare that indicate parturition is approaching. You are a detective trying to solve a mystery: do not ignore what appear to be unimportant "clues." Sometimes the most obscure clue may be a piece that has important significance. However, be aware that some clues may appear out of context, presenting up to a month prior to foaling.

Remember, there are no hard and fast rules. It is impossible to establish a predictable schedule when you are on "Pregnant Mare Time." All, some, or none of the following clues may be evident in your mare in her final 40 days of pregnancy.

Decreased activity level. As her foaling date nears, your mare's desire for activity will noticeably decrease. She may withdraw more and more from social interaction with her pasturemates and you. At times she will appear almost meditative as though focusing all her concentration inward on her changing body and the event that will soon occur.

Your mare may exhibit edema—swelling or "stocking up" in her lower legs—as a result of lack of activity combined with carrying the extra 100–150 pounds of the foal. You may also notice swelling in front of her udder caused by the fetus pressing against and preventing drainage of veins and lymphatic vessels. To rectify the edema, encourage gentle exercise, even if it means hand walking to increase circulation.

In the final month, internal pressure from the growing fetus may even result in the signs of false labor that will present as a mild colic. Hand walk the mare to see if the condition resolves itself. Mild exercise may cause the foal to reposition itself, relieving stress on the mare's organs. If the condition does not improve or increases in severity, call your vet to determine if she truly has colic or is actually going into labor.

Udder changes. The mare's udder will enlarge or "bag up" as the mammary glands become activated in the final two to four weeks of gestation. As foaling becomes imminent, the udder begins to distend, growing firm to the touch. The teats will distend four to seven days prior to foaling. The development of the bag usually occurs over a period of several weeks, but in some mares it happens overnight. The size of the bag may change throughout the day, usually being larger in the morning. Bag development in maiden mares is highly unpredictable as their body has no previous history to follow, oftentimes leaving them to establish their own physical protocol.

Just prior to foaling, the mare also may develop "milk veins" under her barrel as the udder fills. Although called "veins," the condition is really edema that resembles veins extending forward from the udder. It is indicative of a compromised vascular system as are swollen ankles in pregnant women. Although rarely a cause for concern, if your mare exhibits milk veins, it is a good idea to discuss the condition with your vet.

The teats will become full and round, usually beginning to secrete clear droplets of a milk precursor four to five days before foaling. These secretions will change in color and consistency in stages, beginning clear, then changing to a thick, waxy substance to a syrupy amber color and, finally, to a milky white solution.

"Waxing" is the development of early colostrum secretions on the teats in the form of waxy, yellow beads. This condition usually occurs one to four days prior to foaling. However, due to the unpredictability of pregnant mares, some may wax up to two weeks prior to foaling while others not at all. The majority of mares will not foal until their milk has achieved a white composition. When you notice that the milk has turned white, begin 24-hour surveillance. Be warned, though, that some mares may start foaling in the amber stage, quickly achieving the white milk composition by the time the foal is delivered.

A rapid rise in the level of calcium and magnesium in the mare's milk can be noted in the final days prior to foaling. The more concentrated the calcium, the closer she is to foaling. Milk chemistry tests can be conducted using test kits to check the elevating prefoaling calcium content much the same way as checking tap water for mineral content. These tests are efficient, economical and make it easy for the layman to obtain an accurate reading to predict foaling.

Colostrum production. The colostrum is the first milk that the mare produces. It provides the newborn's only source of protective antibodies against disease and infection in his new world. The foal is born without any natural immunity, so it is critical that the colostrum received during its first nursing is of adequate content and quality. The high fat content of the colostrum gives the newborn energy and strength to master the challenges of the first hours of life. It also serves as a laxative to prevent constipation.

Ideally, the foal should receive this life-sustaining substance within the first three hours after birth. Just because your mare has a generous udder does not guarantee the quality of her colostrum. The best on-site way for your veterinarian to assess the quality of your mare's colostrum is with an equine colostrometer or with a clinical refractometer that will measure the specific gravity of the colostrum.

If your mare's colostrum proves to be inadequate or the foal does not nurse, you will need to find an alternative source within eight to twelve hours of birth. Prior to foaling, discuss with your veterinarian possible alternatives such as access to a colostrum bank or using a synthetic product such as Seramune Equine IgG if your mare's colostrum proves inadequate.

Some mares lose milk from their udder prior to foaling. Triggered by hormones, the rate of dripping may vary from slight to streaming. Be careful to record any changes in milk flow as streaming may deplete the mare's source of colostrum before the foal arrives. Streaming may mean that foaling is imminent or it may mean a warning of an adverse condition that the placenta is prematurely separating from the uterus. Whatever the cause, premature streaming should be immediately addressed by your veterinarian to ascertain that the pregnancy is progressing normally or to identify a problem.

Abdominal shape change. Your broad-sided mare's drawn-up abdominal shape will alter in the final two to three weeks of pregnancy, changing from high and wide to low and forward as the muscles in her abdomen relax. In the final days of her pregnancy, the foal will "drop" into position for birth, much the same as in a human pregnancy. Relaxation of the pelvic ligaments of the croup also will be noticeable two weeks prior to foaling, identified by the appearance of a soft, sunken dip on either side of the mare's tail.

Vulvar laxity. This is a gradual process that begins one to two weeks prepartum, culminating 24–48 hours before foaling with a profound relaxation of the lips of the vulva. The vulva gradually loses muscle tone and elongates to accommodate the impending birth.

Temperature changes. Your mare's predictable body temperature will exhibit a slight decrease just prior to foaling. By charting her temperature twice a day beginning at day 300, you may get perhaps your simplest and clearest indication of when the foal will arrive.

Keep a daily log posted on your mare's stall. Be sure to use a digital rectal thermometer because a mercury thermometer lacks the necessary accuracy. When taking her temperature, the tip of the thermometer needs to be in contact with the top of her rectum to guarantee a true reading. Check her temperature at the same time each day, in the morning and evening. It may be easiest to remember if you do your checks at feeding time.

Pending slight increases due to exertion or illness, the mare's temperature should remain constant for each time period checked, reflecting a slightly normal increase in the evening. Within 24 hours of foaling, your mare's temperature will show a slight dip of one-half to one degree. This temperature change may be one of the strongest indicators you will receive that foaling is imminent. Do not ignore it!

Electronic monitors/Contact devices. Some mare owners rely on electronic monitors that are attached to the mare to alert them when foaling is about to occur. When a contact point in the device is broken by a mare's specific movements, a transponder triggers an alarm which is sent to a pager or to a receiver box.

There are two basic types of monitoring devices: external monitors and internal monitors. External monitors take the form of surcingles or halter attachments. They activate when the mare lies completely flat for longer than 10 seconds. Due to the physical stress of late pregnancy, the mare will generally avoid the uncomfortable nature of a flat-out position that stresses her breathing, unless she is in labor.

Internal monitors activate when the foal begins to push into the birth canal. A transmitter is sutured to the lip of the mare's vulva with an activating magnet on the opposite side. Birthing pressure against the vulva will break the magnetic contact, relaying an alarm to a receiver. Insertion of internal monitors requires your veterinarian to perform a minor surgical procedure. However, some mares may become irritated by the device and try to rub it out, which can cause tissue damage and infection.

In theory, electronic monitors appear to be a great idea designed to save you worry and sleep. However, in practice, due to the very nature of their application, they may run the risk of relaying a false labor alarm. There is also the possibility that by the time a foaling alarm is received, it may be too late to rectify a birthing problem such as an improper presentation. Even if your breeding budget can afford the sizeable investment, which may run in excess of $1,000, it does not warrant your unflagging confidence in this type of monitoring technology as there are no fail-safe systems. While they can play a beneficial role in the determination of parturition, your most accurate testing aids may prove to be milk testing and temperature charting.

A remote camera is an excellent monitoring tool that can provide round-the-clock surveillance of your mare. Rather than spending long, cold hours on barn watch, it allows you the luxury of tracking your mare's progress from the warmth and comfort of your home. In addition to monitoring the mare prior to foaling, the remote camera also will provide you with an excellent method to noninvasively survey the newborn's activities during its first days of life.

An inexpensive monitoring alternative system is a standard human baby monitor to pick-up the sounds of birthing that are quite distinct from normal stall activity. Place one monitor outside the mare's stall and keep the other with you as you proceed through your regular daily barn schedule. The range and frequency of the units vary, so be sure to know what your facility requires. These units can be purchased inexpensively at any store selling baby accessories.

Any one of these tools relied upon exclusively may fail you, but used together they will provide a more comprehensive picture of when your mare's actual foaling event will occur. Your best chance of success is a combination of monitoring tools combined with thorough and regular observation.

Despite your best personal efforts combined with modern technology, your mare may still fool you. If this is the case, console yourself that 90 percent of foalings occur uneventfully and do not require human assistance. Remember, your mare retains control of "Pregnant Mare Time."

Personal Journey

By mid-April the bounce had definitely gone out of Anastasia's step. Grazing was her chosen mode of exercise. Trotting across the pasture was beyond consideration. My mare, who had always delighted in rolling in big, thrashing motions, was now forced to stand up to switch sides as her increasing bulk prevented her from flipping over. The highlight of her day was now a deep massage over her back and loins that I would administer when she came in from the field for dinner.

Despite her distorted figure, in my eyes Anastasia never had an ugly day, even in the final weeks. Her black coat glistened from her pregnancy hormones and high-fat diet. The bright sparkle never left her eyes that alertly took in everything in her environment and especially my movements when I was in the barn.

However, I frequently caught her regarding me with a puzzled "Now what?" expression. Much as I hated to admit it, after 30 years in the horse business, for once I didn't have an answer. All I could do was give her a sympathetic, we're-both-maidens-in-this-venture, taking-it-one-day-at-a-time pat. Book learning and educated advice formed a great support network, but nothing could replace firsthand experience of which we had none. We were accumulating our actual experience together one day at a time. It was just the final episode that still remained a mystery.

In late April, a month prior to her due date, Anastasia's box stall was transformed into a 12 foot by 24 foot luxury suite by removing the partition to the adjoining stall. I also removed the rubber mats from the center, exposing the bare limestone base to provide the foal with better traction after delivery. For the time being, I continued to bed the stall with shavings, delaying switching to straw until closer to the foaling date.

Anastasia's only neighbor was my 27-year-old retired Grand Prix dressage horse, Tusquin. As I planned to have him serve as the foal's pasture nanny once it was weaned, I wanted to expose the foal to him from the first day. My mare had always been fond of him and seemed to draw comfort from his naturally calm demeanor. I would catch her dozing in the afternoon, leaning against his stall wall, often with her muzzle touching his through the bars.

When the stall had been expanded, I installed a remote camera that would reveal the entire stall area on my bedroom television. I highly recommend that first-time expectant mare owners invest in this monitoring tool. There are all sorts of enticing gadgets in the marketplace, claiming to alert you to the foal's imminent arrival with buzzers or alarms, but nothing beats having direct visual access to the mare from the comfort of your home at any hour of the day. At the least noise or instinct, the push of a button will display immediate answers on your television screen.

No more semi-dozing in a chair, wrapped in a horse cooler in a cold barn aisle outside the mare's stall. No more panicked runs to the barn on a hunch or a sound. With remote monitoring, your mare can remain undisturbed in relative peace until the picture on the screen alerts you that your foaling-attendant skills are required.

The installation of a barn cam may not save you a lot of sleep, but it will definitely ease the stress of your vigil as well as monitoring the activity of the newborn's early days. The peace of mind derived far offsets the reasonable investment in the equipment, which can be used for countless other stable monitoring situations after the foal is born.

Anastasia was wormed with Ivermectin and received the last of her three EHV-1 boosters on March 15. On April 15, she was inoculated with her regular spring booster shots, including influenza, Eastern/Western encephalitis, tetanus, Potomac horse fever and West Nile. My vet assured me that the foal would receive its initial antibodies against these diseases from my mare's colostrum at first nursing.

On April 19, I began to keep a daily journal to track every detail of the changes in Anastasia's physical status throughout the final month. Even though there were very few changes to record in the first two weeks of charting, it provided a good opportunity to hone my observation skills.

With the exception of some excessive tail rubbing on the stall wall in late April, there were no marked changes in her condition until May 4. That date was the first time that I noticed her udder starting to fill. Her barrel also seemed to have dropped and expanded a bit. On May 6, she was very restless before breakfast, exhibiting excessive tail swishing, stretching and pawing as though she wanted to roll. Initially, it appeared she was verging on colic. However, her appetite was good, and nibbling on hay seemed to take her mind off her discomfort until it passed. This was the only day she expressed any physical anxiety over her condition.

For the next 17 days, her demeanor was quiet and calm. I recorded the increasing physical indications as her belly continued to drop and she began to exhibit hollows in front of her hips. By May 11, there was a distinctive slackening and sinking of the muscles on both sides of her tail.

On May 19, I recorded a marked dropping of her barrel and noticed her udder was much fuller. For the first time, I noticed a small amount of clear liquid on her left teat. Each day her udder continued to enlarge. Her teats also began to fatten and elongate. On May 23, she still remained quiet, but I noticed a greater accumulation of yellowish fluid on both teats.

The twice-daily noted temperature log proved to be my best indication of when Anastasia would foal.

In addition to Anastasia's physical signs, my journal included a daily log of her temperature. She was an extremely good sport for this experiment, never threatening to launch me across the stall when she saw me approaching with thermometer in hand at morning and evening feedings. Though, as the days progressed, the temperature taking became a tedious process for both of us. The readings consistently ranged between 98.5 in the morning to 99.8 at the evening feeding. There was very little fluctuation in the pattern until the evening of May 23. At that time, her temperature dropped dramatically to 97.9 on the evening reading.

The drop in temperature put me on high alert. That clue, combined with a very full udder that was now showing whitish drops of fluid, sounded the warning bell. We were close—very close!

Chapter 9

Ready, Set ... Deliver

The time has finally arrived. The anticipation from 11 months of planning, nurturing and dreaming has reached the much awaited climax. It is hard to tell if you or your mare is more eager for the conclusion of the pregnancy. If you have chosen to assume the responsibility of being her primary foaling attendant, it is time to concentrate and make this role your primary focus in the final days. Be sure you know how to recognize the three stages of labor, when to expect things to happen and what to do when those things occur.

As your mare's designated foaling attendant, be sure you and your facility are as prepared as possible in advance of the big moment to avoid possible life-threatening disorganization. Several weeks prior to your mare's due date, assemble the items that may be necessary to assist her during her labor. Store your foaling kit in a clean bucket in a convenient, dust-free location in the stable so it will be easily accessible when required.

Foaling Attendant Kit

- ❑ Halter, lead shank and twitch.
- ❑ Flashlight with extra batteries.
- ❑ Digital thermometer with flexible tip.
- ❑ Sterile roll cotton, clean buckets and Ivory soap to cleanse the mare's udder prior to delivery.
- ❑ Clean cotton towels to rub down the foal at birth. Be sure they have not been dried with scented dryer sheets which may irritate the newborn.
- ❑ Tail wrap to prevent dirty tail hair from contaminating the vulva during birth.

❑   1–2% betadine solution to treat the foal's umbilical stump.

❑   Shot glass or small glass for betadine stump treatment solution.

❑   Sterile shoulder-length plastic sleeves for use in a vaginal exam if the foal is improperly presented. Obtain from your vet.

❑   Sterile lubricating jelly to lubricate the sterile sleeve if you need to check the position of the foal.

❑   Sharp blunt-end scissors.

❑   Baling twine to tie the placenta to the mare's tail until it is completely passed, so the mare does not step on it and damage her uterus.

❑   Fleet enemas to be given to the newborn to help with the passage of the meconium (first manure). Purchase adult size from the local drug store. Have two on hand in case a second dose is required.

❑   Large, heavyweight trash bags for storage of the placenta until your vet can examine it. Have extra bags for clean up.

❑   Clock, notebook and pen to time and record all birthing activities. Your clock should have a second hand and glow-in-the-dark face.

❑   Portable or cell phone with your vet's number attached or programmed in.

It has been your mission throughout your mare's pregnancy to keep her safe and healthy. Every eventuality within your control has been studied, questioned, thought out and planned. However, as your mare approaches the end of her pregnancy, you will find yourself in a frustrating position, confronted by determining the accurate timing of parturition, which can be highly unpredictable. It is important that you understand and recognize what is a normal foaling versus a dystocia (difficult delivery).

To further confuse the situation, your mare's labor may begin as an intermittent series of distinct or questionable signs that occur over a period of days, or they may present suddenly without warning. Be alert for any abnormal physical or behavioral indications that signal an emergency that requires professional intervention to safeguard your mare and foal. Respect these caution signs: They demand your immediate attention. Formulate a plan of action with your veterinarian for what to do in various scenarios until she can get to your farm.

The preparatory stage of labor is called Prepartum. Your mare will experience an escalation of prefoaling behavior in direct response to the increased physical activity of the foal as it begins to reposition itself in the uterus in preparation for delivery. This condition may require great patience on your part because prefoaling behavior may be evident for several hours to several days prior to the mare entering stage 1 of parturition.

During prepartum, your mare will experience abdominal discomfort, which may present as colic or premature labor. Colic can be ruled out if your mare is still interested in food and is passing feces. Pressure from the foal against your mare's organs may cause her to experience difficulty urinating and defecating, while straining to pass frequent small amounts. Other recognizable prepartum behavior includes glancing at her barrel or restless, mild stall walking. Mares frequently will raise and hold up a hind leg to alleviate the cramping. Face rubbing or yawning, including curling back the upper lip is a normal reaction. She may rub her tail or press her hindquarters against the stall wall. She may hold her tail slightly away from the body.

Do not be overly concerned about your mare unless her behavior becomes extreme or dangerous to her health. As stressful as it may be for you, prepartum behaviorals should be considered a perfectly normal part of the birthing process.

Stage 1 is marked by the physical signs of your mare going into labor. The normal duration is one to eight hours. However, some mares will shortcut the process, passing quickly through this stage in half an hour. A small percentage of mares seem stuck in time, revolving in and out of this stage for days.

If you are present at the onset of stage 1, it is a good idea to call your veterinarian, especially if this is your first experience. Give her a heads-up that foaling activity has begun. Some vets may elect to check in at your farm, while others will request to be kept appraised of your mare's progress by phone. As many foalings occur at the same time of the year, it may be difficult for your vet to be on hand for your mare's event if all appears to be progressing normally.

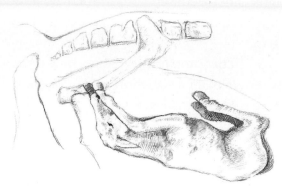

During gestation, the foal is positioned in the uterus on its back with its nose toward the mare's tail.

At the beginning of stage one labor, the foal will rotate from its back 180-degrees in the uterus to reposition itself into the "diving position" necessary for a smooth delivery.

Hormonal changes drive stage 1 as the mare's uterus gears up for the impending birth. Up to this point, the foal has been reclining on its back with its nose toward the mare's tail. Uterine activity in stage 1 cues the foal to begin rotating 180 degrees to reposition itself into the "diving position" required to streamline delivery.

The mare's cervix begins to dilate to provide a sufficient opening through which the foal will pass. Cervical dilation is an uncomfortable process for the mare. While at this point she is still not exhibiting the overt straining contractions of active labor, she will become extremely restless, pawing or pacing her stall. The yawning, face rubbing reflex accelerates. Her raised and extended tail position continues to be a warning signal. She will also swish it in a unique up-and-down flagging action rather than the normal back-and-forth motion. She may frequently lie down and get up. Sweaty patches will appear on her chest and flanks. She will frequently pass small amounts of urine and loose feces.

Then sometimes, in the midst of all this physical activity, it seems that the mare's body throws an "off" switch. Just as suddenly as the restless activity started, the mare becomes totally peaceful, unconcerned with her physical state as she quietly nibbles hay.

If she slips into a calm state, you should take the opportunity to prepare her for the next stage of labor. Wrap her tail, and then wash her vulva and udder with a mild soap. Thoroughly rinse off the area with warm water. When you are finished, apply a clean tail wrap.

Take advantage of this time to clean and rebed her stall with fresh straw. After the mare and her stall are clean, it is best to leave her alone unless she seeks further attention and human comfort. The distraction of people, excess barn noise or the constant turning on and off of lights may sometimes cause the mare to postpone foaling for hours or days. Strive to keep your barn environment as consistent and private a possible.

Caution: If your mare exhibits an elevated level of labor distress for more than several minutes without her water breaking, you need to be on high alert and in contact with your veterinarian. The cause of her distress may be that the foal is misaligned in the birth canal. It may also indicate premature separation of the placenta.

Also called a "red bag delivery," premature separation of the placenta can be immediately recognized by a velvety, red bag bulging out of the vulva instead of the milky white membrane of the amniotic sac. **This is an emergency situation and will not await your vet's arrival.**

The unborn foal's only oxygen supply derives from the placental attachment to the mare. Once the placenta has completely separated, the foal is without oxygen and will suffocate in a matter of minutes unless its head is released from the amniotic sac outside the mare to breathe on his own.

The moment you recognize a "red bag" condition you must use your blunt-tipped scissors or your hands to tear open the bag. This will allow the amniotic sac to push through as in a normal delivery. If acted on immediately, the foal may suffer no ill affects. However, any delay may cause oxygen deprivation, possibly requiring resuscitative efforts. If your vet is unavailable to assist in the delivery, she should coach you through resuscitative techniques prior to foaling day in the event that your foal is delivered with thready, irregular respiration or no breaths at all.

While a "red bag" delivery cannot await your vet's arrival, a misaligned foal with normal placental attachment who has not broken through the placenta can wait for your veterinarian to conduct a vaginal exam to determine the best way to proceed. To forestall further labor, it may help to keep your mare up and walking until the vet arrives. Movement of the mare also may be beneficial in helping the foal to self-correct its birthing position for a normal delivery.

Stage 2 begins with the breaking of the mare's water and lasts through the delivery of the foal through the birth canal. Stay calm and focused during this stage as things will happen very quickly, requiring your utmost concentration. The average length of stage 2 is 15–30 minutes with 40 minutes considered the outside range of normal. Be sure to check your watch as soon as the water breaks to time your mare's progress through stage 2. Chart the progression of birthing activity in your stallside journal to keep an accurate record for your vet in case of complications.

The mare's water breaks when the foal's front hoof pushes against a natural weak spot on the placenta at the cervix called the cervical star. This action ruptures the outer placental sac (allantois-chorion) which has served as a conduit for the foal's nutritional and oxygen requirements during the pregnancy. The rupturing of the outer sac releases several gallons of allantoic fluid that provides lubricant for the smooth passage of the foal through the birth canal. The outer sac is red with a velvety texture. In normal births, it is ultimately delivered inside out (red side in) at the end of the birthing process in the form of the placenta.

Once the outer placental sac ruptures, the foal remains encased within an inner second sac called the amnion that does not rupture at this time. The amnion is recognizable as a thin, slippery, whitish fluid-filled membrane that cushions the fetus while in the uterus.

Throughout stage 2, the mare will exhibit very restless behavior, getting up-and-down as she seeks to alleviate her discomfort. Many mares break their water while in a standing position. Unlike the act of squatting to urinate, when the water breaks the mare will be fully standing or in the process of lying down where her forehand will lower before the hindquarters. In some mares, the allantoic fluid is expelled in a resounding rush, while in other mares, the water may initially break as a trickle and does not gush until she lies down or until the bubble-like amniotic membrane appears.

There should be approximately a five-minute window between the water breaking and the presentation of the whitish amniotic sac through the vulvar lips. The foal's front feet should be visible through the sac with the soles facing down.

Caution: The positioning of the hooves or their absence is the visual cue to whether this is a normal delivery or an emergency. Malpresentation will require veterinary advice or assistance. If you suspect a problem, get your mare up at once and keep her moving until you contact your veterinarian. It should be noted that your first glimpse of the hooves prior to the presence of the head might be soles up. However, your mare's actions through rolling or getting up and down may cause the foal to retract back into the birth canal where it may reposition itself by rolling over into the diving position required for proper delivery.

A perineal laceration can occur from a foal who is presented incorrectly. In this scenario, the foal's hoof escapes the birth canal to perforate the mare's uterine and rectal wall. The result is a hoof that protrudes from the mare's rectum rather than from her vulva. The delivery must not be allowed to continue as your mare will sustain severe damage from tearing. Try to delay the delivery until your vet can arrive to assist. Get your mare up and moving immediately in the hope that the foal's hoof will retract into the birth canal.

Though rare, there are a variety of improper presentations that can occur during stage 2. They will usually require veterinary intervention. In this instance, your biggest contribution toward a healthy delivery is to keep your mare up and in motion until your vet arrives.

In a correct presentation, the second forehoof should appear a few inches behind the leading hoof. This offset position allows the foal's shoulders room to clear the mare's pelvis. During the delivery, you may notice the forelegs push out through the vulva then retreat back inside, controlled by the waves of contractions that are strongest at this point. Each contraction will expel the forelegs a little farther out.

At this point, your mare may appear unsettled, getting up and down as the foal progresses through the birth canal. In her effort to find the ideal birthing spot, she may wander the stall. Try to prevent her from damaging the foal's protruding legs because she may accidentally bump them against the stall walls as she moves around. Be careful that she does not lie down with her hindquarters pressed against a wall without leaving room for the foal to pass. If she crowds a wall, you must get her up again so she can readjust to a safe delivery location with her vulva at least 3 feet from the nearest wall.

The mare may lie down for the final time when she begins to deliver the foal's head. Expect to see the foal's muzzle atop its knees when they finally appear. If the head does not appear, get the mare up and walk her to see if the head will reposition. If it does not self-correct within five minutes, call your vet. In the meantime, keep the mare moving to stall delivery. If the head position resolves itself through your efforts, allow the delivery to proceed as normal.

As the foal's head and shoulders pass through the birth canal, the amniotic membrane should tear. If the exposed muzzle remains covered by the sac, carefully tear the thin membrane away from the nostrils with your fingers to allow the foal to breathe free of fluid. You may need to clear any mucus that is blocking the nostrils.

By the time the head appears, the mare usually remains lying down until the delivery is completed within 5–30 minutes. Waves of contractions 15–30 seconds apart will next deliver the shoulders. This is the most difficult stage due to the spatial limitations of the mare's pelvis. You should see forward progress with each contraction. The passage of time for this phase of delivery should be carefully monitored.

Caution: An exceptionally large foal or a condition of the mare called uterine inertia in which the mare ceases to have contractions may cause delays during this phase. If your vet's not present, either condition may require you to assist your mare under the guidance of your veterinarian's coaching over the phone.

If your vet feels that assistance is warranted, be sure to follow your mare's lead. Pull on the foal's legs only when she pushes and rest when she rests. Be sure to pull out and down toward the mare's hocks to follow the natural arc of the birth canal.

Once the shoulders have been delivered, it is natural for the mare to rest before completing delivery of the foal's hind legs. The healthy newborn will roll up on its chest within 15 minutes. If it does not, you will need to prop it up and support it with your knee until it can support itself. Excessive fluid accumulates in the foal's lung lobes that cannot be cleared when the newborn lies flat at birth for an extended period of time. Inability to clear the fluid can predispose the foal to pneumonia.

At this point, the foal should be breathing on its own at an average rate of 60 breaths per minute. Be sure its nasal passages are clear of mucus and debris to allow the unrestricted passage of air. To clear its nasal passages, begin just beneath the eyes and firmly swipe your fingers down the length of its face, finishing at the nostrils, to drain out any fluid. If the foal is still not breathing, vigorously rub its body with a clean towel or straw to stimulate respiration and the foal to breathe on its own.

Caution: If the foal does not respond by taking a breath or exhibits very slow respiration, lay the foal flat on its side and proceed with mouth-to-nose resuscitation. This is accomplished by closing off the foal's mouth and one nostril with your fingers. Blow vigorously into the open nostril, exhaling as large a breath as possible. When you exhale, the foal's chest should rise. Be persistent, supplying regular, strong breaths as the technique may take several minutes to be effective. Mouth-to-nose resuscitation is a good technique to maintain a borderline foal until your vet arrives.

During the rest period while the mare and foal are still down, the umbilical cord exchanges beneficial blood from the placenta to the foal. **Do not attempt to cut or break the cord.** Natural movement between the mare and the foal should cause the cord to break at a weak point about one inch from the foal's abdomen. There will be minimal bleeding at the natural breakpoint. However, should the foal's umbilical stump continue to bleed or hemorrhage for one or two minutes after the cord breaks, grasp the stump between your thumb and fingers to apply pressure until the bleeding subsides. If bleeding persists, your veterinarian will need to address the situation.

When the cord does break, the umbilical stump should be saturated as soon as possible with betadine or a 0.05 percent chlorhexidine solution from your foaling attendant's kit. Do not directly dab the betadine solution on the stump with cotton as the tissue is very fragile and may bleed from contact. As cotton can easily shred, dabbing may leave material fibers on the stump. Also, do not spray the solution on a colt as you can burn his penis. The best technique is to pour the solution into a small glass and "dunk" the stump for 30 seconds. Care must be taken to properly disinfect the stump at birth because it can be a primary site for the entrance of infection into the foal.

At the end of the rest period, the foal will struggle to extricate himself from the mare or the mare will stand, finishing the delivery.

Stage 3 is the recovery period that begins after the foal has been delivered. It usually lasts anywhere from 30 minutes to three hours. This stage is marked by the mare passing the placenta and fetal membranes through postpartum contractions. They should be totally passed within three hours of delivery.

At this point, the mare begins to experience uterine involution, the natural shrinking process that gradually contracts the uterus to its prepregnancy size. This condition will continue over several days. The uterine contractions will cause the mare physical discomfort in the form of cramping that may become severe. She may appear mildly colicky, swishing her tail or picking up her hind legs. Even her facial expressions may show her displeasure with her condition. Her self-absorption with the pain may distract her focus from the newborn at a time when you would expect her to be most attentive. This is particularly true of maiden mares.

Before administering any anti-inflammatory drugs to ease your mare's discomfort, confer with your veterinarian to be sure you are not masking a more serious, even life-threatening condition. There is a big difference between uterine involution discomfort and the profound pain of a more serious problem such as uterine artery rupture or true colic.

Caution: Under normal circumstances, the uterus completely separates from the placenta as the afterbirth enters the birth canal to exit through the vulva. If complete separation does not occur such that any part of the placenta remains attached to the uterus, the weight of the evacuating placenta can pull the uterus out of the mare.

This unfortunate, rare condition is called uterine prolapse. It is easily identified as a protruding red mass. The initial visual presentation is small, increasing in size as the uterus turns inside out as it tries to leave the mare's body. Your veterinarian should be notified immediately. While you are waiting for her to arrive, support the uterus from slipping any farther out of the mare by constructing a sling from a bed sheet wrapped around the mare to protect her uterus.

Do not try to physically assist the mare in the passage of the placenta. There is absolutely **no** reason for you to pull on it. Manual assistance in the passage of the placenta may result in uterine prolapse. The mare's own efforts combined with gravity will eventually complete the job. To prevent the mare from stepping on the placenta until it passes, tie several knots in the dangling mass above the level of her hocks to keep it off the ground.

Caution: If the placenta tears before complete passage, pieces may be left inside the mare that may damage her uterus. Retained placental matter can result in uterine infection and subsequent laminitis. If the mare has not passed the placenta within three hours, it is important to notify your veterinarian.

Injections of oxytocin may need to be administered to assist the uterus in releasing the placenta. Note that the oxytocin dosage listed on the bottle is greatly higher than the dosage your veterinarian will prescribe. Confer with your vet prior to administering this drug. High levels of oxytocin may result in extreme uterine contractions that can cause uterine prolapse.

When the mare has passed the placenta, save it for your veterinarian to examine for any abnormalities. A normal placenta will weigh approximately 10 percent of the foal's birth weigh, so it may be awkward to handle. Store the placenta in a feed sack or heavyweight trash bag that can be sealed off until the vet arrives.

You may notice your mare also passes a tannish-brown, fist-sized mass at the same time as the placenta. This is the hippomane. At first glance, it may resemble a misplaced organ. However, there should be no cause for concern. In reality, the hippomane is a collection of discarded uterine debris formed into a mass during the course of the pregnancy with no further function.

Personal Journey

4 a.m., May 24…I awoke from a deep sleep. I don't know what awakened me. It could have been one of the horses in the stable giving a restless nighttime kick or it could have been intuition. Whatever the reason, I instinctively switched on the television to check Anastasia on the barn cam.

It was easy to see her because I left her stall light on overnight for the past two weeks in case the foal arrived early. All previous overnight checks had found her dozing contentedly nose to nose with my old campaigner in the adjoining stall. She had always appeared calm, which meant I was calm which saw us through another peaceful night.

May 24 was different. Although Anastasia did not exhibit overt signs of distress, her behavior pattern had definitely changed. The first thing I noticed was her stretching and twisting her neck while expressing big yawns. Occasionally, she would flag her tail up and down rather than normal side-to-side swishing. As I watched, she would pace a lap of her big stall then settle down again next to Tusquin to doze for a few minutes.

The pattern repeated, but without increasing regularity or distress. Even though I was wide awake and anxious to be with her, I decided that at this early stage, my presence in the barn staring worriedly into her stall would probably be more disruptive than helpful. Forcing myself to stay put, I continued to monitor her on the television, remaining as patient as possible.

6 a.m.…Anastasia added mild, irregular kicks to her repertoire of yawns, stretches and tail flagging. There could be no mistake. Stage 1 labor had definitely begun. I shook my husband awake as I headed for the stable, pausing just long enough to call my vet to leave a message that Anastasia was in Stage 1.

The eight residents of my stable were pleasantly surprised to see me an hour early for breakfast. Stomach clocks easily adjusted as they began to bang and nicker. Feeding chores quickly completed, I set about preparing Anastasia for her big day. She seemed to appreciate the extra attention, which briefly took her focus off her impending condition. While I gave her a thorough grooming and washed her udder, my husband stripped her stall and rebedded with fresh straw.

By the time we had finished our chores, Anastasia was noticeably dripping milk, even streaming at times. I tried to collect and save some of the milk in case she was losing colostrum, but my novice efforts resulted in very limited success.

7:30 a.m.…In the hope that an early morning graze in the sunshine would ease some of Anastasia's growing discomfort, I turned her out in the small paddock that adjoined her stall. As I leaned on the fence watching her nibble grass, it truly hit me in that moment of peace that this beautiful mare who I so loved was about to deliver the foal that I had been planning for four years. All my wishes, hopes and dreams would be realized—or not—in the next few hours.

Suddenly, it seemed that the 338 days since Anastasia had conceived had flown by far too quickly. I had spent the time productively studying countless textbooks as well as asking veterinarians and experienced breeders a myriad of questions. I had recorded all my findings and experiences in a carefully crafted journal that had become my trusty roadmap through this journey. All that research and supportive data had sounded very convincing for the past 337 days.

But now, watching my very pregnant mare graze, I was confronted by the harsh reality that this was the day that she would deliver a foal. As her foaling attendant, I had a role to play—possibly a very major role. Now faced with that truth, all my studying and writing seemed worth no more than the paper on which it was written. How could the book learning of a maiden breeder with a maiden mare replace actual hands-on foaling experience, of which I had none?

My ideal vision of foaling had centered around my confident, experienced vet taking charge of the process while I looked on with admiration and assisted where needed. However, when Dr. Strosnider returned my call at 7:45 a.m., I realized that my ideal vision had burst. "Sounds like you're going to have a foal today," he confirmed. "Call me when it hits the ground."

"You mean you can't come now?" I asked with disbelief. "This rookie is not ready. I need the first-string team."

"I'm too far away on another call, but I'm sure you'll do just fine," he encouraged. "Remember, it's a natural process. Just keep a close watch and let Anastasia do her job. Keep me posted. I'll swing by your farm around 11."

He was gone. I was not reassured.

8 a.m....Filled with growing doubt and anxiety, I called Meredith to update her on Anastasia's and my status. If anyone could talk me through this experience, it was Meredith, who had been my advisor and font of information throughout the entire breeding process.

Meredith answered on the second ring, her voice conferring instant calm, directing my rising uncertainty into logical thought and action. If Meredith, my teacher, thought I was capable, then maybe I was.

"So, tell me what is she doing right now?" she urged after I had summarized the events that had occurred since 4 a.m.

Anastasia was still peacefully nibbling grass, occasionally giving a little kick or flagging her tail. "Not a lot has changed in the last two hours. Maybe she's a little more restless, but nothing major."

"Keep a close eye on her," Meredith advised. "It sounds like she's almost ready. When she breaks a sweat, you're just about there."

8:15 a.m....As I looked a little closer, I realized that the morning sun had begun to reflect a gleam of damp sweat on her neck, which had been dry just moments before. As Anastasia turned to snatch a new patch of grass, I noticed some drops of fluid expel from her vulva, which had become greatly elongated from the previous day.

"Wonderful!" Meredith exclaimed in response to my findings. "You're about to have a foal! If you don't want it to be born outside, I suggest you get that mare back in her stall right now."

I hustled Anastasia back into the barn just as my helper, Becca, arrived for work. "Run to the house and get Doug. Tell him to bring the camera. Our foal is on the way!"

Stage 2 labor struck at warp speed, much faster than any book or advisor had led me to believe. Events were unfolding so quickly that there wasn't time to be nervous. There was only time to react and marvel at the miracle of birth.

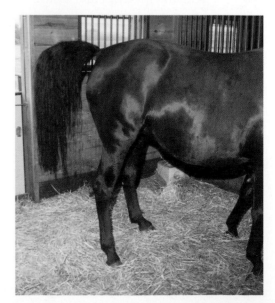

Anastasia's water breaks as soon as she is brought in from pasture at 8:20 a.m.

As soon as the water breaks, the amniotic sac and the first tiny hoof appear while Anastasia is still standing.

8:20 a.m.….Anastasia's water broke. She remained standing, sweating and panting through the contractions. Almost immediately, the amniotic sac bulged through her vulva. I held my breath until, through the thin membrane of the sac, I could see a tiny hoof with its sole facing the ground indicating a correct birth presentation. With each forceful contraction, a bit more of the foal was revealed. Four inches beyond the first hoof, a second appeared followed by a petite nose with a pink tongue pushed out the left side of the mouth.

The sac had not broken, so I gently tore it open to expose the foal's nostrils which immediately began to draw breath. I noticed the hair color was brown, answering one of the big questions of the past 338 days.

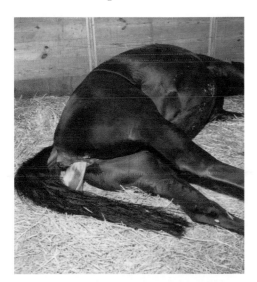

Anastasia lies down to finish the delivery as the second hoof appears.

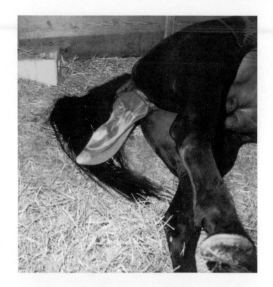

The appearance of the second hoof is quickly followed by the foal's muzzle.

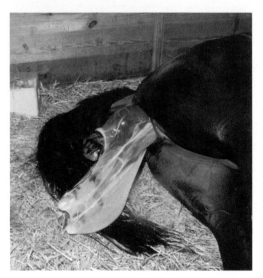

The foal began to draw its first breaths of air as soon as the amniotic sac was broken to expose its nostrils.

With the foal's body still covered by the sac, Anastasia pauses for a brief rest period before the hind legs are delivered.

With the head exposed, Anastasia sank to her knees with a groan, flopping onto her left side. She was very efficient in her contractions, expelling the foal in less than three minutes.

8:25 a.m.…The long-awaited foal has arrived! The back half of its body was still encased in the sac so we still had no idea whether it was a colt

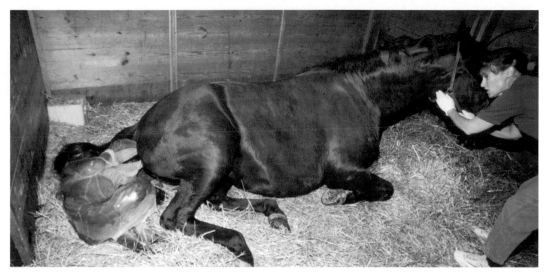

I calm and steady Anastasia to prevent her from rising too rapidly before the foal is completely delivered.

or a filly. The foal was breathing rhythmically and appeared healthy, so I said a little prayer of thanks. I ran my hand down the front of its face beneath its eyes to its nostrils to clear any remaining mucous, but the airways appeared unrestricted. Gently, I put my fingers to the tiny muzzle, which immediately stimulated the suckle response from the foal's little lips.

Overcome by exhaustion, both mare and foal took a break. Anastasia lifted her neck to curiously survey the tiny brown shape that lay behind her. Flaring her nostrils, she gave a very soft, gentle nicker. In that moment, I sensed, with relief, that my maiden mare's maternal instincts had awakened.

Anastasia stands as soon as the delivery is completed while the foal rests in the straw behind her.

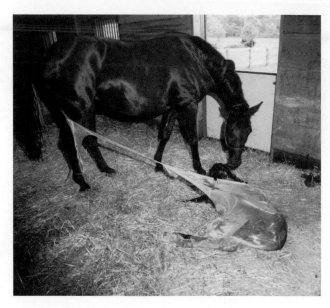

Anastasia turns to curiously touch her newborn for the first time. The cord stretches to its natural break point.

The nicker seemed to trigger her need to stand. She surged to her feet with amazing ease considering what she had just been through.

As she turned, the cord broke cleanly without hemorrhage.Instinctively, she gently stretched her neck out to investigate the tiny bundle that she had carefully carried for over 11 months.

Still partially covered in the sac, the foal rolls up on its chest and tries out its front legs for the first time.

8:30....Unassisted, the foal rolled up onto its chest. Amazingly, only five minutes had passed between the water breaking, the foal being delivered and my mare back on her feet cleaning her newborn. Talk about efficiency!

Anastasia bonds with her newborn as she explores and cleans her.

Anastasia emitted contented, throaty nickers over her foal that almost sounded like she was purring. I was in awe of the power of nature's instinctive programming. It was amazing that she knew exactly what to do, exhibiting far more expertise than me who was marveling from the side of the stall in a state of suspended animation at the process.

For a beautiful moment, time truly did seem to stand still.

The two curious new mothers get acquainted with our eagerly anticipated arrival.

Chapter 10

Newborn Expectations

Once you get past the awe-factor tears that cloud your eyes on delivery, it is time to get down to the serious business of inspecting the newborn. The newly delivered foal will take some time to rest behind its dam as it tries to get a bearing on its very foreign new environment. This window of calm represents an ideal opportunity to conduct a brief physical exam, checking the foal's temperature, pulse and respiration to ascertain that things are proceeding normally. The physical condition of a newborn can change rapidly, so it is essential to immediately identify and respond to any life-threatening abnormalities.

You should recognize that your newborn is alert with accelerated respiration and heart rate. Do not be surprised that normal neonatal respiration is very rapid, averaging 60–80 breaths per minute immediately after birth with an accelerated heart rate up to 130 beats per minute on standing.

To check the foal's heart rate, put pressure on the lingual artery at the bottom of its jaw where it crosses the bone. Count the pulse rate for 15 seconds, then multiply by four to approximate the heart rate. For a more accurate reading, you can also use a stethoscope, listening to the left side of its chest behind the elbow.

You may notice your newborn's gums and the sclera of the eye are a very bright pink. This coloration is a natural condition caused by the accelerated heart rate. The color will recede as the heart rate slows. After the first hour, the foal's heart rate will decrease to average 80–100 beats per minute. Within an hour, the respiration should also drop to 30–50 breaths per minute when resting.

Neonatal foals tend to exhibit a slightly elevated temperature of 100–102 degrees. This is perfectly normal for a newborn. Expect the temperature to fall to the normal 100-degree range within one hour of birth. However, newborns who run a low temperature below 98 degrees are cause for concern because they are experiencing hypothermia. Your first clue before even taking the temperature will be obvious shivering. Immediately rub the foal with towels to provide warmth and stimulate increased blood flow. Keep the foal covered with a blanket until your vet arrives.

The newborn's initial head and body movements may appear jerky or spastic as it receives massive sensory input. This is a perfectly normal reaction that will calm as the foal begins to adapt to its surroundings.

Do not be surprised by the appearance of the newborn's hooves. At birth, the bottom of the hooves will be covered by rubbery, fingerlike projections designed to protect the walls of the uterus as the foal passes through the birth canal. These projections will wear off during the foal's early attempts to stand.

It is the mare's job to clean her newborn, so avoid the temptation to dry off the foal unless she ignores it or it appears very cold. The smell and taste of the newborn form an important part of the bonding process for the mare. Your interference at this point may hinder bonding to the point of rejection particularly in maiden mares. *Recognize when and if you are needed.* If the foal is breathing normally and resting comfortably, this is a good point to step back and enjoy watching the discovery process going on between your mare and her foal.

This pause in the action is also a good opportunity to quietly remove the soiled birthing bedding from the stall so the foal has a clean and dry base as it begins its attempts to stand. Slippery floors will frustrate its initial efforts, resulting in exhaustion and possible injury.

If you choose to imprint your foal, the closer to the moment of birth this is started, the better. Imprinting as described in Dr. Robert Miller's popular book, *Imprinting the Foal,* is a process of repetitively touching the foal in key areas to desensitize it to stimuli that may be unpleasant later in life. This process is believed by many to help foals be more tractable for procedures such as farrier and veterinary work. Basic imprinting techniques include gently probing the mouth, ears and anus, tapping the bottom of the hooves and rubbing the entire body.

Within 20–30 minutes of birth, the foal should exhibit the suckle reflex. You should notice the tip of a healthy pink tongue protruding from the front of its mouth. Initially, the newborn will randomly suck on anything that comes in contact with its lips. You may want to occasionally check its mouth for any inedible objects, such as straw, that may accumulate from its suckling efforts.

Initial attempts by the foal to move its legs will be extremely uncoordinated. It may take up to an hour of trial and error for the foal to struggle to stand. Many sport horse foals have extremely long legs that often require a bit longer to organize.

You may find it stressful to watch your newborn's early efforts to master the coordination necessary to stand. However, these early struggles have the beneficial effect of stimulating circulation. The foal's early disorganized movements will cause a continual loss of balance, resulting in repeated tumbles. Do not be overly concerned with this natural process because your foal is very flexible and rarely injured in the process. If your foal has not achieved upright balance within an hour of birth, you should notify your veterinarian as it may indicate a neurological problem.

Caution: Neonatal maladjustment syndrome or "dummy foal" is believed to be a consequence of lack of sufficient oxygen to the foal's brain during delivery. Initially, a foal afflicted with NMS will appear normal, but abnormal neurological signs will appear within the first hours of life. Symptoms include wandering aimlessly, barking, loss of the suckling reflex and/or seizures. This is an emergency situation that requires immediate veterinary attention.

Try not to become physically involved in the action taking place in the stall until your foal discovers the balance to stand. However, if you feel the foal is becoming fatigued or frustrated by its efforts, you may want to help stabilize its uncertain balance by supporting its body with a cradling hold. Be aware that some warmblood foals may weigh in excess of 150 pounds, so be prepared for a challenging balancing act.

Proper cradling of the foal is done with one arm wrapped around the front of its chest and shoulders. Take extra care not to block its windpipe, which is very fragile. The other arm should surround the foal's hindquarters above its hock and below its tail. Keep your face close to the foal to avoid a sharp rap on your head by the foal's poll as it struggles for balance. Avoid supporting the newborn around its rib cage because too much pressure in that area can cause serious damage such as rib fractures that can puncture or collapse a lung. Cradling should only provide light support as the foal needs to learn to develop independent balance as soon as possible.

Enjoy the small victory when your foal finally achieves independent, stationary standing balance. However, the struggle will begin anew once it tries to walk. The initial forward attempts will be excessive, resulting in a backward overcompensation with subsequent loss of balance. If you are providing cradling assistance to your foal as it tries to walk, your best strategy is to position yourself near its flank. Foals tend to fall backward, so you may be able to catch and provide some stabilization support. Regardless of your best efforts, you will be unable to prevent frequent falls as the newborn learns its balance parameters.

The foal's genetically programmed goal at this point is to move toward the mare to seek nourishment. She may nicker encouragement and even assume an accessible physical stance, but often she is a bit self-absorbed, focusing more on the discomfort of her uterine contractions or satisfying her own post-birth appetite with hay.

If possible, before the foal nurses for the first time, clean the mare's udder of any dirt and bacteria that have accumulated during the birthing process. Use only warm water, avoiding soap. The warm cleansing also may help to ease the tenderness the mare is experiencing from a very full, swollen udder. First nursing can be very uncomfortable for the mare, especially a maiden who does not understand the process and may relate the foal's efforts to the source of her pain.

When the foal finally achieves standing contact with the mare, it will exhibit the suckling reflex on any and all parts of her body with which its mouth comes in contact. Although the foal's uncoordinated efforts may be very frustrating to watch, avoid the temptation to assist during its early attempts. If possible, it is best to allow the mare and foal to work things out on their own. The mare often will help the foal by nipping it on its hindquarters to direct it back toward her udder. The foal may take some time to discover and successfully latch on to a teat, all the while struggling to maintain upright balance.

Maiden mares may require some extra care and patience. If the mare refuses to allow the foal to nurse, you will need to exert some restraint. With a handler at her head, position her hindquarters in a corner of the stall. Then hold up her near front leg so she cannot kick the foal or you. If she still resists, you may need to use a twitch. Always use the least amount of restraint necessary to solve the problem since you are already in a high stress situation.

Caution: On rare occasions, a mare may reject her foal to the point of inflicting grievous physical harm. This behavior may occur in maiden mares who are confused and distressed by the discomfort and unfamiliarity of the birthing process. Mares experiencing pain from a difficult delivery also may reject their foals. This behavior first becomes apparent with the foal's initial attempts to nurse tender teats on a swollen udder.

Be on high alert for signs of rejection behavior because they can have dangerous consequences for you as well as the newborn. Carefully read the mare's body language and facial expressions which can be very telling. Low level rejection is exhibited by the mare posturing aggressively toward her foal, and biting and kicking to warn it away. A more advanced stage of rejection actually can result in the mare savaging the newborn.

Low-level aggression may be resolved by restraining or distracting the mare until she learns to accept her foal. It may initially take several assistants to divert the mare's energies while positioning the foal to nurse.

In more extreme cases, your vet may need to assist you with chemical calming agents for several days to allow the bonding process to occur. During this time, the mare and foal should be separated by a partition that allows them to see and smell each other while protecting the foal from the mare's aggressive tendencies. It is the handler's responsibility to bring them together on a normal nursing schedule round-the-clock until it is considered safe to leave the foal unattended with the mare.

In the case of a mare who does not accept her foal despite your best efforts, it may be necessary to find a surrogate nurse mare or, if unavailable, hand-raise the foal as an orphan. Mares who display irreconcilable rejection behavior tend to repeat the pattern with future foals. Serious consideration should be given as to whether or not to rebreed this mare.

It is essential that the foal nurse successfully within three hours of birth in order to receive the life-sustaining antibodies found in the first milk—

colostrum. The sooner the foal receives colostrum, the better. It is important that the newborn ingest approximately 32 ounces of colostrum within the first eight hours of life in order to gain protection from bacteria and infection.

If the foal does not nurse within the first three hours, you may need to milk the mare to get the colostrum directly into the foal. The newborn's digestive system is only receptive to ingesting the colostrum antibodies for a limited time, achieving peak absorption 12 hours after birth. The ability to absorb antibodies ceases within 24 hours of birth, so the timing of this crucial step is essential.

Prior to nursing, it is good practice to check the specific gravity of the mare's colostrum to ascertain that it is of sufficient quality. This can be done with a refractometer or colostrometer. However, these instruments are an expensive investment especially if you only have one mare. Ask your vet to check with her equipment.

If your mare streams milk causing premature lactation prior to the foal's first drink, it is important to test for colostrum quality. If the quality is lacking, absent or your foal does not nurse, you will need to have access to an alternate source of colostrum from a frozen colostrum bank or a synthetic product such as Seramune Equine IgG. Just to be safe, establish a back-up colostrum source plan with your veterinarian prior to your foaling date.

The synthetic Seramune Equine IgG can be given orally or intravenously. Oral Seramune should be administered via nasogastric tube within the first 12 hours of life while the foal's gut is still open to assure absorption of protective antibodies. It is a safe product with an excellent performance record if it's used within the 12-hour window. On the other hand, if you miss the 12-hour window, intravenous Seramune can be administered to the foal when the gut is no longer absorbent. However, IV Seramune does carry a slight risk of a fatal anaphylactic shock response which is not a problem with the oral product.

Caution: If your foal does not stand within one hour and/or nurse within three hours of birth, call your veterinarian because your newborn may be at risk of developing foal septicemia. This condition is a potentially fatal bacterial infection of the bloodstream caused by ingesting bacteria or the invasion of bacteria through an open wound such as the umbilical stump.

Initially, the newborn may only nurse for short spurts, interspersed with rest periods for sleep and energy renewal. Expect the normal newborn to nurse every 20–30 minutes, draining the mare's udder with each meal. If the udder appears continually engorged, it is a warning sign that the foal is not gaining sufficient nutrition through proper nursing. Take note if the foal's face is wet with milk because this may be an indication that it is experiencing a poor suckle reflex or having difficulty attaching to the teats.

The newborn should receive an enema if it has difficulty passing the meconium. This first manure is a dark, sticky stool with a hard core that forms in the foal's colon prior to birth and it is typically passed within a few hours of foaling. The meconium may create a blockage that is difficult for the foal to pass without assistance. Agitated tail swishing and visible straining can be damaging to the foal if the condition is not alleviated.

In most cases, the enema should be administered after the first nursing to ease the passage of the meconium. However, some foals will not nurse if distracted by the impaction. If the foal abandons nursing because it is so fixated on the discomfort of constipation, you should give an enema at that time.

Warm the commercial phosphate enema to body temperature by immersing it in warm water prior to inserting it in the foal's rectum. You may also warm the enema by heating it in a microwave for six seconds. Be sure to shake the enema to ensure equal heat distribution. Check the temperature of the liquid on your wrist before inserting into the foal.

Lubricate the tip of the enema with Vaseline or KY jelly prior to inserting. Have an assistant stabilize and restrain the foal with a cradle hold. Gently insert the tip of the enema into the foal. Squeeze the enema to empty the contents into the foal, being very careful not to damage the rectum which may be very tight. You will probably notice a dark meconium stain on the tip of the bottle when you withdraw it.

The response to the enema usually occurs within 10–15 minutes. When all the meconium has been passed, the stool will turn to a soft, mustard-colored composition. If the first enema is nonproductive and the foal continues to strain, administer a second dose. If a second enema does not produce relief, call your veterinarian because the foal may have a blockage that cannot be resolved by an enema.

If your veterinarian was not on hand for the delivery, she should visit the mare and newborn as soon as possible to conduct a complete physical exam on both horses. She will check heart rate, respiration and temperature as well as gum and eye color. The mare will be examined for any damage or tearing caused by the birth. She will also check the mare's placenta that you have saved to make sure it has passed in its entirety.

In the foal, she will additionally check the suckle reflex, limb angulation, the umbilical stump and note any physical abnormalities such as cleft pallet or parrot mouth. Many foals' legs are less than perfectly straight at birth. It may take several days for the deviation to correct itself. The degree of abnormality should be assessed by your veterinarian who will determine if any correction is required. Based on the degree of irregularity, your veterinarian will develop exercise parameters, which should be carefully monitored for the first few days of life.

She should also draw blood from the foal to test the IgG level to ascertain that the foal has absorbed sufficient life-sustaining antibodies from the mare's colostrum. In order to accurately test the level of absorption, the test should not be administered until the foal is 12 hours old. On the test results, you are looking for an acceptable IgG level above 800 mg/dl. A level of 400–800 mg/dl is considered questionable with further supplementation a consideration. A reading below 400 mg/dl is poor and should definitely be addressed by your veterinarian with therapeutic treatment.

While a clean bill of health on the exam is reassuring, you will need to remain watchful. The status of a newborn's physical condition is extremely fragile and can rapidly deteriorate for no obvious visual reason. The sooner you catch and address any changes in condition, the easier they are to rectify and prevent future damage. For the moment, take a deep breath and be satisfied that you have made it to this point, but be advised it is necessary to stay on high alert for the next few hours and days.

Personal Journey

8:35 a.m....Amid encouraging nickers from Anastasia, the foal made its first fumbling attempts to rise. My husband gently slid the remainder of the sac from the foal's hips and hind legs. Although he claimed he did it to make movement easier, I think his real motive was to end the suspense over the gender of the foal.

While the foal rests from the rigors of birth, I do an abbreviated form of imprinting, gently running my hands over her entire body.

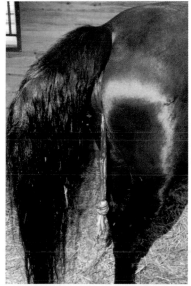

Until Anastasia could naturally pass the placenta, I tied it up above her hocks to prevent her from stepping on it while she moved about the stall attending to her newborn.

It's a filly! A precious, petite filly with the same beautiful dished head as her mother and her grandsire, Edinburg. The only marking was a perfect small star between wide-set eyes that accentuated her lovely head.

While she was resting quietly I took advantage of the moment to do an abbreviated type of imprinting. Cooing in a low droning tone, I softly ran my hands across her entire body, then tapped the soles of her tiny hooves. Finally, my fingers gently probed her ears, nostrils, mouth and beneath her fuzzy tail. Her reaction was calm and accepting of all physical contact.

8:45 a.m....Anastasia was exhibiting strong contractions to pass the placenta. I quickly tied up the dangling mass above her hocks to keep her from stepping on it as she moved restlessly around the stall focused on her foal.

Amazingly, only 30 minutes earlier, she had been grazing in her field, but now she was totally absorbed with her newly delivered foal, encouraging it to stand.

8:48 a.m....The foal announced her presence with a shrill whinny. It was the first hint of the resilient spirit possessed by the bundle of spunk that had just entered my life. I was so amazed that such an incredibly strong sound could be emitted from such a small creature still damp from birth. The whinny was so full of life, proclaiming to the world that she had definitely arrived. As if we hadn't noticed!

With the whinny came renewed, highly motivated attempts to stand. Spread eagle, belly flop, side flop. I was witnessing an amazing display of the indefatigable spirit of life as failed attempt upon failed attempt did not for a moment deter or diminish her efforts to stand.

9:23 a.m....Obstacles to movement finally overcome, the foal wobbled atop uncertain legs for the first time. Triumph only one hour after birth!

Anastasia passed the placenta. It appeared to be intact, but Doug and I put it in a trash bag and stored it in a can outside the stall for Dr. Strosnider to examine when he arrives.

9:40 a.m....The foal is down again, flat out, exhausted from the struggles of trying to coordinate and untangle her ungainly legs. This appeared to be the ideal opportunity for us to treat her umbilical stump to prevent infection. Doug steadied her body while I carefully dipped the exposed stump into a small glass filled with diluted chlorhexidine. The foal had an instantaneous negative reaction to the sting of the fluid, violently expressing her displeasure by squirming away from us to struggle back up on unsteady legs. It was a surprising display of strength and determination from such a delicate, little creature.

The foal's first attempts to stand were met by the challenge of organizing four unstable, long legs that each seemed programmed with a different coordination.

Anastasia provided maternal encouragement for her newborn who rests after a belly flop in a failed attempt to stand.

9:50 a.m....Those unsteady legs seemed to have found their bearing for, without warning, she wound up and expressed her joy of new life with an incredible capriole mid-stall, landing square on all four feet. Quite a feat after only 85 minutes of life!

With the foal appearing to make positive progress, I turned my attention to Anastasia who appeared to be growing increasingly uncomfortable from uterine involution contractions. One moment she was physically frustrated, kicking out in pain, while the next she was trying to track her newborn around the stall. Her continued personal discomfort would not permit her to settle long enough in one place to allow her to relax so the foal could connect to nurse.

I was my foal's biggest cheerleader as she finally achieved a fragile mastery of her balance.

Anastasia's growing self-absorption with the discomfort of uttering involution caused her to lose focus on the foal when the waves of pain became strong.

10:25 a.m....My vet had still not arrived to examine the foal, but I had been in regular phone contact with him since the birth. At his suggestion, I administered Anastasia paste Banamine to help ease her physical discomfort, and allowing her to focus on her foal.

The filly exhibited a strong suckle reflex, but she was having difficulty connecting with her mother's udder. Being a maiden, Anastasia appeared quite concerned when she could not see her foal. Whenever the filly would move back toward her udder, Anastasia would spin around to keep the foal in her line of sight. There seemed to be no end to this dance.

11:30 a.m....Three hours had passed since the birth, but despite the foal's best efforts, she had still not nursed. The entire team, human and equine, was exhausted by the effort. The clock was ticking down on our limited window for the filly to ingest the all-important life-sustaining colostrum. Much to my dismay, her bright sparkle seemed to be fading right before my eyes and there did not appear to be anything we could do about it.

12 p.m....Dr. Strosnider arrived to conduct a thorough exam. On first examination, he gave the mare and foal a good basic health report. However, he was concerned that the color and consistency of Anastasia's milk indicated that she had already passed her colostrum, leaving none for the foal who had yet to nurse. He confirmed our suspicion that the heavy milk streaming that

Anastasia and I comfort the foal who, after 3 hours of life, was visibly weaker from her early exertions. Her exhaustion was compounded by her failed attempts to nurse which had prevented her from ingesting any nourishment or colostrum.

Anastasia had exhibited two hours prior to foaling must have depleted her colostrum supply.

12:15 p.m....Dr. Strosnider decided to administer 200 ml of Seramune Equine IgG to the foal via nasogastric tube. This was going to be a very tough, invasive procedure for the newborn; however, there did not seem to be an alternative to resolve our colostrum dilemma.

Despite the foal's diminutive size, the task required all available hands to accomplish the job. Dr. Strosnider and Jeannie, his vet tech, as well as Becca, Doug and I, all held a piece of the foal, mare or equipment. Ultimately, with much thrashing and restraining, we succeeded in getting the product tubed into her small body. Despite our momentary triumph, we would not know if the synthetic product would ultimately provide the same protection as her mother's natural colostrum until the next morning when Dr. Strosnider returned to run an IgG test.

As a final safeguard, Dr. Strosnider dosed the foal with electrolytes because she appeared dehydrated from lack of nursing. To add insult to injury, we also administered an enema to help her pass the meconium that was block-

ing her intestinal tract, causing her to strain. Despite receiving some immediate relief from the enema, she continued to strain sporadically.

1:30 p.m.…The meconium blockage was still causing the foal discomfort. I administered half of a second enema. Almost immediately, the foal tried
to force out a large meconium plug without success. Doug reached in with a
finger lubricated with Vaseline to give her a manual assist that ultimately
resolved the problem and finally ended her straining.

2:00 p.m.…Foolishly, I had thought that the textbook delivery of a
healthy, beautiful filly meant that we were home free. However, her failure to
nurse was developing into a great frustration for me. I was quite concerned that
nearly six hours after birth, she still had not succeeded in nursing. She had
suckled on everything within reach except her mother's teat. Despite the
Banamine treatment, Anastasia's engorged udder and uterine pain made her
progressively uncomfortable and unresponsive to the foal's searching efforts.
Mare and foal were equally frustrated. Being a maiden breeder, this problem far
exceeded my expertise, so once again, I turned to Meredith.

Despite her busy veterinary practice, she had told me that she would be
on call for me all day to assist however she could via telephone. She was
emphatic with her current advice: "You definitely must get that foal to nurse
as soon as possible. If they haven't figured out the routine on their own by
now, you need to step in. Have someone position the foal at the mare's flank
near a teat. Someone else needs to
milk directly into the foal's mouth.
You may have to repeat this routine a few times, but once the mare
and foal get into a pattern, they
should be ok on their own. Be
patient and firm. I know you can
do it. Good luck!"

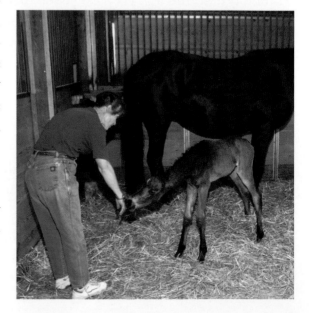

2:10 p.m.…Armed with my
assignment and renewed determi-

*The foal eagerly succeeded in suckling on
everything, including my hand, except for
Anastasia's udder.*

nation, I gathered my team of Doug and Becca in the stall. Becca stationed herself at Anastasia's head to prevent her from walking away or swinging around to look at her foal. Doug cradled the foal firmly at the mare's left flank, positioning her active lips toward a teat. I carefully reached under my mare's belly from her right flank. Taking a teat firmly between my left thumb and index finger, I tried to squirt some of the abundant flow of milk into the foal's eager mouth.

Pressure from a very full udder made Anastasia quite irritable and kicky in response to my hand actions. It required all of us to do some very creative fumbling and repositioning to stay connected. However, patience and perseverance finally paid off with a stream of milk finally hitting its target between the foal's lips, followed by a big swallow. I swear at that moment I heard bells chime!

2:20 p.m....Appetite quenched, the foal dropped down at her dam's feet to nap in the straw, exhausted from the strenuous activity of finally nursing. Flat and motionless, she slept heavily while Anastasia stood guard over her tiny body.

I was concerned that Anastasia was neglecting her own physical needs due to her intense focus on her newborn. She hadn't taken a drink of water or shown interest in food since the foal was born. While the foal napped, I took advantage of the lull to go outside and pull some of the long, lush grass that grew along the barn fenceline. The sight and scent of it immediately perked up Anastasia who eagerly accepted one of her favorite delicacies from my hand without hesitation. Sensing I had hit on the solution, I sent Becca back out to the fence to fill up a bucket. Whatever Momma wants, Momma gets!

2:35 p.m....The foal popped up and immediately focused on nursing. Anastasia still appeared uncomfortable and unsettled. As she was obviously not ready to take charge, I re-called my nursing team for Round 2. Becca resumed her position at Anastasia's head while Doug stabilized the foal and I worked the teats. Our system resulted in another successful effort. Although Anastasia's restless shuffling and twisting, combined with the foal's fumbling efforts, convinced us that we were not ready to let them nurse solo, we were certain that we had developed a workable system that with time and patience would ultimately resolve the problem.

2:45 p.m....On completion of nursing, the foal immediately lay down to nap again. Anastasia resumed her watchful guardian position over her. Despite her growing acceptance of the foal, I could tell she was still experiencing great personal discomfort from uterine involution. I administered another 1,000-pound dose of Banamine paste that finally seemed to ease her pain.

2:55 p.m....The foal scrambled up from her short nap and immediately headed directly for Anastasia's flank. Since she appeared so determined, we decided to eliminate the role of teat handler, but kept Becca at Anastasia's head while I directed the foal's body toward her goal. It was an immediate success. I felt just like Henry Higgins in *My Fair Lady:* "By George, they've got it. I think they've got it!"

The rest of the afternoon fell into a regular rhythm of nurse-play-nap, repeating at approximately 40-minute intervals. I stationed myself on a tall director's chair just outside the stall, keeping watch and making notations in my journal to log all activities and changes. I rested when they rested, assisted when they needed help.

3:30 p.m....By this nursing session, I was the only required handler. The only necessary action was for me to stand quietly at Anastasia's head to prevent her from turning to face the foal. She finally seemed to comprehend the system, realizing that it was not imperative to always turn toward her foal. The regular nursing routine seemed to have eased some of the pressure on her udder, which made her more comfortable and relaxed. I sensed she was

Mission accomplished after 7 long hours and a crew of assistants, the foal finally nurses on her own. The 3:30 p.m. nursing was the last time I was needed to stand at Anastasia's head as she finally understood and accepted the procedure.

exhausted from the exertions of the day, but still she remained intensely vigilant, standing over her foal, gently nuzzling her whenever she slept.

7:00 p.m....They were nursing confidently, unassisted by human contact, acting like two old pros. While Anastasia's uterine discomfort seemed to have finally subsided, I was concerned that except for the hand-pulled grass, she had not eaten or taken a drink for nearly five hours. I administered 25 cc of oral paste electrolytes in the hope of stimulating her desire to drink.

9:30 p.m....Anastasia finally took her first, long drink of water, nearly draining her water bucket. A few minutes later, she walked to the far side of her stall and urinated. What a relief to see her systems finally getting back on a normal track.

11:00 p.m....In the dim illumination of a single light bulb, mother, daughter and "grandmother" were jointly exhausted. However, I diligently maintained my post, lulled into the peaceful rhythm of nurturing and bonding that filled the stall. The maternal force that was binding my young mare to the tiny brown bundle at her hooves was hypnotic. Whenever the foal was asleep, Anastasia delicately groomed every inch of her delicate frame, exploring each body part with the pure amazement of first touch. At one point, she carefully took a tiny front hoof between her lips, held it for a moment, and then gently replaced it on the straw with a noticeable sigh.

Despite the lateness of the hour and the fact that I had been on high alert in constant surveillance mode since 4 a.m., no power on earth could make me leave the stall front. The experiences of the past 19 hours had been both overwhelming and pure magic. And suddenly I knew what was the obvious and only appropriate name for my beautiful new foal who had captured my imagi-

With birth, wobbly legs and nursing miraculously mastered, Vivaldi's Magic settled down to sleep at the end of her first day of life, content and relaxed as though she had always been a permanent resident of Full Cry Farm.

nation and the essence of this moment as she lay sleeping peacefully at her mother's feet—Vivaldi's Magic. The realization of my dreams, the promise of all that could be, my fresh beginning with a bright future ahead.

Postscript

On August 31, 2004, Vivaldi's Magic was presented at the Swedish Warmblood Association of North America breed inspections held at Lake Erie College in Painesville, Ohio. The filly did me proud, mirroring her dam's elegance and maturity in the ring despite a crowd of curious spectators and very unfamiliar surroundings. In front of the judges, Magic handled herself with amazing obedience and confidence for a 3-month-old inexperienced foal off the farm for the first time. The judges awarded her inspection bonit scores of 8 for type, 8 for head/neck/body, and 7 for gaits, for a final score of 23 points to earn a Class 1 rating.

As the head judge pinned the blue Class 1 ribbon on Magic's tiny halter, I basked in the significance of the moment. It marked the culmination of my odyssey that had begun nearly five years earlier with my first sight of a 5-month-old Anastasia galloping boldly in her mother's shadow across a windswept Swedish field. Despite the twists, turns and challenges, I would not have traded a moment of my journey.

There have been offers for Vivaldi's Magic from prospective buyers interested in her bloodlines or captivated by her type and charm. However, I think she will remain in residence at Full Cry Farm, stabled next to Anastasia, so I can find out how the next chapter of my magical journey turns out. The possibilities are endless.

The culmination of years of planning and dreaming, Anastasia and her mirror-image daughter, Vivaldi's Magic, boldly look toward fulfilling the challenges of the future that awaits us.

Glossary

acremonium. The mold strain present in some fescue that may cause pregnant mares to abort when ingested.

allantoic fluid. The fluid between the outer and inner placental sac that is released when the cervical star ruptures.

allantois-chorion. The outer placental sac that attaches to the lining of the uterus.

amnion. The inner placental sac that cushions the fetus while in the uterus.

anaphylactic shock. A rapid allergic reaction to an antigen that may progress to a life-threatening condition.

anestrous. The period of the year when the mare is non-reproductive.

artificial insemination (AI). Injection of semen into a mare by means other than sexual intercourse.

bonit scores. Scores awarded at a Keuring by appointed breed association representatives for various specifics of conformation and movement. These scores become a part of the horse's permanent record.

breed-back policy. Contract terms to rebreed to a specific stallion if a pregnancy does not occur. The contract will specify the length of time that the policy will be honored as well as any additional charges.

breeding soundness exam (BSE). The examination and laboratory testing of a mare for determination of reproductive fitness.

caslick. Surgical procedure to close the dorsal (top) half of the vulvar lips to prevent contamination of the uterus from urine, stool and air. It is reversed near foaling time.

catch. Slang term for "becoming pregnant.

cervical star. The natural weak spot on the placenta at the cervix.

cervix. Muscular ring of tissue that separates the uterus from the vagina.

cleft palate. A birth defect of the upper palate that creates an opening between the oral and nasal cavities.

colostrometer. A device for measuring the specific gravity of colostrum to determine if sufficient antibodies are present.

colostrum. The first milk produced at birth that contains protective antibodies.

contagious equine metritis (CEM). A highly contagious bacterial disease that is initially spread by sexual transmission from the stallion to the mare. It causes infection and inflammation of the mare's genital tract.

corpus hemorrhagicum (CH). The structure formed immediately on release of the egg as the follicle fills with blood.

corpus luteum (CL). The structure formed from the mature corpus hemorrhagicum that produces progesterone, the chemical responsible for maintaining pregnancy.

deslorelin. A synthetic hormone given to induce ovulation.

diestrus. The period in the mare's estrous cycle when she is not capable of becoming pregnant.

dystocia. A difficult delivery.

early embryonic death (EED). A variety of disease processes that cause the death of an embryo in its early development.

edema. The swelling of an area of the body with fluid.

embryo. A fertilized egg.

embryo transfer. The harvesting of an embryo from a donor mare at approximately seven to eight days post-ovulation. The embryo is then transferred into a recipient mare who will maintain it for the duration of the pregnancy.

embryonic vesicle. The fertilized embryo including the surrounding fluid and membranes.

encephalitis. An inflammatory disease of the brain.

endometrial cups. Structures formed in the pregnancy after day 40 and disappearing by day 150. They secrete the hormone eCG, necessary for embryo maintenance.

endometrial cysts. Thin-walled, fluid-filled lymphatic or glandular changes in the lining of the uterus.

equine viral arteritis (EVA). Contagious viral disease spread as a cold or venereal disease that may cause abortion, fever, respiratory disease and limb edema in pregnant mares.

equine herpesvirus type 1 (EHV-1). Abortion-inducing strain of equine-herpesvirus.

equitainer. The brand of fresh-cooled semen transporter container made by Hamilton Research, South Hamilton, MA.

estrous. The period of the year when the mare is hormonally reproductive.

estrus. The period in the mare's estrous cycle when she is in heat and releasing an egg that can be fertilized.

extender. Fluids of various compositions used to dilute collected semen prior to shipping.

FEI. Federation Equestre Internationale. The international governing body of equine performance sports.

fescue. A pasture and hay forage that can cause reproductive failure in mares if contaminated by acremonium mold.

fetus. The developing embryo.

fistula. An unnatural opening between two body surfaces or organs, such as the one caused by the improper delivery of a foal's foot, penetrating the walls of the mare's vagina and rectum.

foal heat. The mare's first heat post-foaling, usually 9-10 days after delivery.

follicle. The egg-containing structure in the ovary.

genotype. The genetic makeup of an individual.

gestation. The period of time from fertilization of the egg through birth.

human chorionic gonadotropin (hCG). A drug used to induce ovulation.

hippomane. A collection of fetal refuse formed during the course of the pregnancy that is passed with the birth of the foal.

IgG level. A blood test to determine the amount of antibodies in the newborn foal's bloodstream.

imprinting. Repeated touching of a newborn in key areas to desensitize it to stimuli that may be unpleasant later in life.

infectious placentitis. Any infection of the placenta.

inspection. The inspection and grading of breeding stock by judges appointed by specific breed organizations.

live foal guarantee. A breeding contract benefit that waives the stud fee for rebreeding to the stallion if a live foal is not produced.

malpresentation. The incorrect positioning of a foal, resulting in an abnormal delivery.

meconium. The first fecal material passed by the newborn foal.

milk testing. A diagnostic test to check for escalating calcium levels in the mare's milk prior to foaling in an effort to identify the time of parturition.

morphologic evaluation. The microscopic examination of sperm cells for normal versus abnormal shapes.

motility. The movement of sperm as examined under a microscope.

neonatal maladjustment syndrome (NMS). A collective term for progressive neurological abnormalities that may be observed in a newborn foal as a disease process.

osteochondrosis dessicans (OCD). Skeletal disorder characterized by abnormal flaps or loose pieces of cartilage within a joint.

ovulation. The release of an egg from the ovary.

oxytocin. A drug used to cause uterine contraction.

parrot mouth. A defect of the mouth whereby the upper teeth protrude over the lower teeth in an overbite.

parturition. The act of giving birth.

perineal laceration. The tearing of the soft tissue around the vulva and perineum of the mare during birth.

phenotype. Physical appearance of a visibly identifiable genetic trait.

photostimulation. Variations created in daylight duration, either naturally or artificially, that trigger hormonal changes in a mare.

platter feet. Very flattened, spread-out hoofs, shaped like a platter.

polyestrous. Exhibiting more than one estrus cycle. Mares are seasonally polyestrous, having more than one estrous within the breeding season.

progesterone. The hormone that maintains pregnancy.

prostaglandin. The hormone that controls the development and ovulation of follicles.

prepartum. The period prior to birth.

private treaty. A private breeding contract that allows the stallion owner flexibility in setting his stud fees and mare requirements that may vary with each individual situation.

progeny. Offspring.

rectal palpation. The veterinarian's gloved arm is inserted through the rectum into the colon of the mare to feel the size and shape of various parts of the reproductive tract and subsequent pregnancy.

red bag delivery. Premature detachment of the placental membranes during parturition, appearing as a velvety, red bag protruding from the vulva.

short cycle. The administration of hormones to shorten the length of the estrous cycle so that breeding can be performed sooner than would otherwise naturally occur.

Stamm number. A number assigned to a mare line to track the progeny through the female descendents.

straw. A small tube for the storage of frozen semen.

streaming. The continuous release of milk from the mammary glands without the stimulation of suckling.

studbook. The registry of a specific breed association.

suckle reflex.. The automatic response to suck that is exhibited by a newborn foal.

teaser. A gelding or stallion whose close physical presence elicits heat displays in a mare to test her readiness for breeding.

theriogenologist. Veterinary specialist in the field of reproduction.

tipped vulva. A conformational defect whereby the upper portion of the vulva is tilted inward allowing stool from the rectum to contaminate the vagina.

ultrasonography. Diagnostic tool utilizing soundwave echoes to visualize internal body structures.

uterine horn. The section of the uterus between the ovaries and the uterine body in which the fetus grows until birth. The uterus is equipped with two horns, but the fetus occupies only one.

uterine inertia. The fatigue of uterine contractions such that they become weak, ineffective or stop altogether.

uterine involution. Uterine contractions to expel the placenta and subsequent shrinkage of the uterus to return to normal shape.

uterine prolapse. The expulsion of the uterus inside-out from the body through the vaginal opening.

uterine tone. The degree of firmness of the uterus.

uterine torsion. A twisting of the uterus on its axis within the mare that obstructs proper blood flow to the uterus.

Verband. German organizations that oversee the registration and inspection of breeding stock. There is a separate Verband for each of the German warm-blood areas, e.g., Hannover, Holstein, Oldenburg, etc.

vulva. The external genitalia of the mare.

vulvar laxity. The elongation and relaxation of the external vulva prior to parturition.

waxing. The development of early colostrum secretions on the teats in the form of waxy, yellow beads.

Bibliography

Adkins, Pat. "The Right Start." In *Equus*, Issue 319 (May, 2004).

Beeman, G. Marvin. "Foaling – A Practical Guide to the Foaling Process." In *Western Horseman* (March, 1992).

Blanchard, Terry L.; Brinsko, Steven P.; Love, Charles C.; Rigby, Sherri L.; Schumacher, James; and Varner, Dickson D. *Manual of Equine Reproduction*. Second Edition. St. Louis: Mosby, 2003.

Cable, Christine. "Preparing for Foaling." In *The Horse* (February, 2004).

Card, Claire E. "Management of the Pregnant Mare." In *Equine Breeding Management and Artificial Insemination*. Juan C. Samper, ed. Philadelphia: W.B. Saunders, 2000.

Darling, Kjersten and Griffin, James M. *Veterinary Guide to Horse Breeding*. New York: Howell Book House, 1999.

Foley, Cynthia. "Technology Saves Sleep Before Foaling." In *Horse Journal,* Vol. 7, No. 1 (January, 2002).

Hayes, Karen E.N., *The Complete Book of Foaling*. New York: Howell Book House, 1993.

Jones, Theresa. *Complete Foaling Manual*. Grand Prairie, Texas: Equine Research, Inc., 1996.

Maver, Suzanne. *Foaling: Mare & Foal Management*. Australia, Equine Educational, 1995.

McBane, Susan. *Modern Horse Breeding*. Guilford, Connecticut: The Lyons Press, 2001.

Metcalf, Elizabeth S. "Insemination and Breeding Management." In *Equine Breeding Management and Artificial Insemination*. Juan C. Samper, Ed. Philadelphia: W.B. Saunders, 2000.

Schweizer, Christine. *Understanding the Broodmare*. Lexington, Kentucky: The Blood-Horse, 1998.

Samper, Juan C. "Artificial Insemination." In *Equine Breeding Management and Artificial Insemination*. Juan C. Samper, ed. Philadelphia: W.B. Saunders, 2000,

Index

About the Authors

Leslie McDonald is a 40-year veteran of the horse industry. She owns and operates Full Cry Farm, a full-service private dressage training facility in Batavia, Ohio. Leslie has earned the US Dressage Federation's Gold, Silver and Bronze medals for merit in the competition arena for Training Level through Grand Prix. In addition to her 24 years as a dressage instructor and trainer, Leslie had a long career in "A" circuit hunter/jumpers as well as combined training. She is a popular dressage clinician and speaker.

Meredith Weller, DVM, has been a sport horse breeder since 1996, specializing in the development of Holsteiner jumpers at her Meridian Farm in Delaware, Ohio. Offspring from Meridian Farm are currently competing successfully in the hunter/jumper area. A feline practitioner since 1985, Meredith established The Cat Doctor in 1992, a veterinary practice devoted exclusively to felines.